T.S.Eliot

T.S. ELIOT
The Philosopher-Poet

Alzina Stone Dale

Harold Shaw Publishers
Wheaton, Illinois

Printed in the United States of America.

Cover art ©1988 by John Babcock

ISBN 0-87788-832-9

Library of Congress Cataloging-in-Publication Data
Dale, Alzina Stone, 1931–
    T.S. Eliot, the philosopher poet.

    (The Wheaton literary series)
    Bibliography: p.
    Includes index.
    1. Eliot, T.S. (Thomas Stearns), 1888–1965—
Philosophy.   2. Eliot, T.S. (Thomas Stearns),
1888–1965—Religion.   3. Philosophy in literature.
4. Christian poetry, American—History and criticism.
I. Title.   II. Series
PS3509.L43Z66185   1988   821'.912   88-4457
ISBN 0-87788-832-9

97 96 95 94 93 92 91 90 89 88

10 9 8 7 6 5 4 3 2 1

To my aunt
Gay Batchelder Kramer
"Home is where one starts from . . .
A time for the evening under lamplight
(The evening with the photograph album)."
T. S. Eliot, Four Quartets

Contents

Acknowledgments

Many people in England and America helped in writing this book. Mrs. T. S. Eliot took time to write me that she was glad I wanted to deal with the religious side of her husband's life and work since it was usually avoided or deprecated by those who wrote about him. She kindly made it possible for me to see special collections otherwise restricted.

Brother George Every, Professor Sanford Schwartz, and Ted Welch let me interview them, while Marie de Rachewiltz, Anne Ridler, James Brabazon, and William Griffin answered my queries by mail.

A very special group of friends undertook the role of reader-critics: Dr. Corbin Carnell, Dr. E. Richard Gregory, Dr. Catherine Kenney, and Mary McDermott Shideler. Their comments were invaluable. My former Divinity School teacher, Dr. Nathan A. Scott, Jr., also contributed comments on the work in progress and gave me one of his books I'd had trouble finding.

A group of libraries were most helpful in locating books, sending me Eliot correspondence, or making resources available to me in person: the Beinecke Rare Book and Manuscript Library at Yale University, the Department of Special Collections at the University of Chicago's Library, the Bridgman Public Library, SWELP (the Southwestern Educational Library Project), and the Wade Center at Wheaton College Library.

Finally, I want to thank Luci Shaw for suggesting a fascinating project, and Stephen Board and Ramona Cramer Tucker for helping me carry it out. My family, Chuck, Betsy, Alec, and Ken, deserve high praise for accepting my preoccupation with T. S. Eliot during the 1987 Christmas season.

Alzina Stone Dale
St. Valentine's Day, 1988

PART ONE
Puritan 1888 – 1914

Prologue

J. Alfred Prufrock among the Prophets

September 26, 1988, is the centennial of the birth of T. S. Eliot, and this study is a celebration of his life and work from a Christian perspective. Too many readers and critics divide Eliot into three parts: public poet, private man, and (as a kind of embarrassed afterthought) orthodox Christian. The result is a lopsided caricature instead of a rounded portrait of the greatest poet of the twentieth century.

This book was written, first, to show that Eliot was a whole person, not one of his "Hollow Men." In our psychology-oriented era, Eliot's work is interpreted more and more in terms of his life. The emphasis is put on his tribulations, not on the triumph of his Christian beliefs. John E. Booty of the University of the South was right when he said that "in the end, the problem of the poet and the problem of the man coincide." But Dean Booty also recognized the truth of Thomas Howard's comment that because Eliot was a *twentieth-century poet*, most commentators believe that his Christianity ". . . looks suspiciously like an attempt on his part to dodge the tough realities of modern life and to hide amongst Old Testament or Medieval bric-a-brac."

Second, this book was written to encourage Christians to read Eliot as a guide to our times. The shape of his life shows a clear turning, or conversion, that affected his life and work much the way a similar experience affected his contemporary, C. S. Lewis. Like Lewis, Eliot's words speak to our condition; as Nathan A. Scott has shown, Eliot's writings typify the twentieth-century's literary concern with existential or religious issues. In Eliot's case his work has the added value of "modernity," which makes him a poet able to bridge the gap between believers and nonbelievers.

In such a short book it has not been possible to quote Eliot extensively. My hope is that after meeting Eliot here, the reader will seek him out. In describing Eliot and his work, I have tried to follow the criterion of Samuel Coleridge, one of Eliot's ancestors as a poet philosopher: to be a sympathetic critic. I have used the testimony of his friends and associates as often as that of critics and enemies. Above all else, I have taken Eliot at his word, except when he himself was mischievously "rewriting" his own early opinions.

To be asked to draw a portrait of one of the dead masters of the Christian affirmations has been an awesome responsibility, accompanied by Eliot's "moment of primitive terror." But I found an appealing, highly intelligent, shy, and serious-minded man, with a hidden fondness for friendship and fun, one who spoke in the voice of a major prophet.

I found that T. S. Eliot—although often described as his own model for "J. Alfred Prufrock," a diminished twentieth-century man—was among the Christian prophets of our age. Eliot's writing was modern, but he was also the twentieth-century's principal champion of the moral imagination. As Russell Kirk described him, Eliot was the spokesman for a right order in the soul and a right order in the commonwealth. Eliot's ancestors in this quest were Plato, Virgil, St. Augustine, and, above all, Dante.

Like his contemporaries and acquaintances, Lewis, Charles Williams, and Dorothy L. Sayers, Eliot lived within the precincts of the Oxford Christians' City of God. Eliot, too, was a passionate preserver of the Christian tradition, one of those who called themselves "dinosaurs" or "Old Western" men, who refused to discard the past.

At the same time, Eliot as poet presided over the "Age of Eliot." Lines of his poetry have become part of our language. Paradoxically, it was by virtue of his literary stature that Eliot (as he wrote about G. K. Chesterton) helped to maintain "the existence of [the Christian] . . . minority in the modern world." Eliot prepared the way for our post-1984 world, in which despite dire predictions neither religion nor the state has withered away.

The purpose of this book is to reintroduce T. S. Eliot to readers who read his work in school but rarely return to it now. To understand Eliot the poet, it is important to place him in his time, but also to examine his spiritual odyssey. Eliot saw his task as a Christian writer to find a way to reproclaim the Christian faith in terms the modern world could accept.

In the world of literary reputations, however, he is both honored and vilified as a revolutionary poet who became a reactionary prophet. As Howard has pointed out, modern commentary has taken up three attitudes toward Eliot: critics are either embarrassed, avuncular, or urbane. All three approaches patronize Eliot's beliefs and blunt his assault on us.

The "problem" of T. S. Eliot comes partly from our post-Christian sense of a world where Tolkien's eucatastrophes never happen, and partly from the way we write biography. Rarely is a writer taken at his word, or is his public behavior considered the most significant part of his life. Far from engaging in hagiolatry, psychological muckraking has become the respected intellectual norm. We do not read the lives of the great to emulate them, but rather to cut them down to size.

Eliot himself declared that there was no reason why biographies of poets should not be written, provided that the biographer did not add "conjecture about inner experience" to the facts. There is always something about a poem, he added, that cannot be explained by its origins. But present-day biographers insist that biography is our Victorian novel, in which we want to discover our own personalities and define our times. A biographer therefore has the right to manipulate his subject's life and interpret the work to reflect the biographer's own point of view.

When "hanging out dirty linen" is the characteristic of the serious biography, Mrs. Eliot, her husband's literary executor, has shown remarkable faith with the spirit of his wish for no official life. As a reward, she has seen endless studies that use malicious gossip, guilt by association, and Freudian or Marxist psychology to explain away her husband's poetic genius and Christian beliefs.

Exploring his life, I discovered someone who took himself to be a sinner but had many of the hallmarks of a saint—although in his wryly diffident and humorous way, Eliot would have been the first to deprecate such a classification. But Eliot's public loyalty and Christian commitment, private self-discipline, and generosity far outweighed his personal idiosyncrasies.

On a more personal level—like Eliot, I was born into an American Middle Western family proud of its New England Puritan origins. Like Eliot, I was sent east to school, only to find that I was not an easterner. Like Eliot, I was then drawn to Europe, especially to my English roots, but eventually realized that I was really an American. Finally, like Eliot, I was also converted to the faith of my English ancestors. As an Episcopalian, I do not mistake the church's teachings and beliefs for a personal and idiosyncratic construct by Eliot.

As a person, Eliot is usually described as a rather dry, prissy, poetical critic. His career is usually divided neatly in half, with the first half getting the most attention and the second half considerable criticism. Abroad as a rebellious expatriate, Eliot wrote his great dirge to modernity, *The Waste Land*; then he backslid into being a reactionary Christian and monarchical medievalist, a kind of twentieth-century monk.

Those two halves of Eliot never quite meet. They also ignore the whimsical, humorous side to his character, with which he enjoyed elaborate practical jokes and produced the clever and witty verse of *CATS!* (At the same time, a large part of the commercial success of *CATS!* is said to come from parents anxious to say they have taken their children to something written by the great poet T. S. Eliot.)

Although he is still taken seriously as *the* philosopher poet of the twentieth century, most critics still find it easier to make sense of the young Eliot, poetic spokesman of the "Lost Generation," the contemporary and equal of Yeats and Pound and Joyce. In the groves of academe the disillusionment, despair, and madness of a Virginia Woolf are still more fashionable and taken to be more significant than any sort of faith. To add to the confusion of the ordinary reader, some critics insist that it is possible to explain Eliot as the sociological product of his time. Others declare they can understand Eliot's social and intellectual attitudes without accepting them, deliberately separating the poet's writing from his beliefs. Still other critics believe that Eliot began writing poetry as a religious quest, which found a home in Christian orthodoxy. Others, using his early, unpublished poems, say Eliot had a failed vocation to be a martyr, which led him to the Church of England as second-best.

Although these critics take his Christianity more seriously, once Eliot joined the Church they lose interest in his "routine life of prayer and observation," the kind of life which C. S. Lewis called "ordinariness." Virtually none of his critics describe how Eliot merged his Christian and literary priorities to end his life as a beloved elder statesman, in love and charity with his neighbors around the world.

The fact that critics try to diminish Eliot's Christian message by calling it polemic does not make Christianity untrue. One hundred years after his birth it is still difficult to assess the importance of a poet of his stature standing up for Christ. If in his early poems Eliot caught the boredom and impotence of the century, then he took on the daunting task of testifying to spiritual concerns that his world had lost the capacity to imagine.

For readers who do not assume that conversion to orthodox Christianity is a step backwards, the story of T. S. Eliot is a fascinating parable for our times. Like Dorothy L. Sayers, Eliot wanted his work to stand for itself. But his work has biographical elements and can be described as a kind of spiritual autobiography, a mode of writing Eliot had a long-cherished ambition to explore.

As a writer and as a person Eliot can serve as a guide whose quest for spiritual meaning aids our own. His relationship to other twentieth-century Christians also needs describing. Eliot might enjoy having posterity remember him as the librettist of the gaudy musical *CATS!*, but he does not deserve to be summed up as the one who described the modern waste land, and then relapsed into childishness to escape it. His work should be read in the context of mature Christian belief.

CHAPTER ONE

Roots

T. *S. ELIOT WAS TO WRITE THAT THE FAMILY BACKGROUND OF A MAN* of genius was always of interest, especially if the man thought that his ancestry was important to his career. Late in life Eliot benignly admitted that his own American cultural inheritance was crucial both to his life and his work. In 1961 he told a New York interviewer that his poetry had more in common with his contemporaries in America than England, and that its sources and emotional springs came from the United States.

Eliot tempered that remark by adding that his poetry was not what it would have been if he had been born in England, and it would not have been what it was if he had stayed in America. Like Joyce, Yeats, and other famous expatriates, distance from home had given Eliot's work a special quality. In his case, it had also made his heart grow fonder.

Eliot can best be understood in terms of his inheritance and upbringing as an American Puritan of English stock. Since Puritan ancestry and certain American places were formative influences in his life, it is appropriate that Eliot should be called an American writer. Most critics acknowledge this fact, as does the U. S. Postal Service, which recently included him in its literary series.

To call Eliot and his family Puritans, two centuries after the English Civil War and the Puritan heyday in New England, means that Puritan religious and cultural values still prevailed within his family circle and were used to raise the young. Both the Puritan idea of government as a social contract mutually subscribed to and Puritan individual religious fervor were a part of this inheritance.

At different times and places Eliot was to rebel against the Puritan demands but also to identify with his birthright. Both his social thought and his creative work show that he was trying to create a *new whole* that was acceptable to the twentieth century.

Originally the English Puritans were zealous to purify the usage of the Elizabethan Church of England. The Puritan considered the Church of England unable to help him live a godly, righteous, and sober life of self-examination and spiritual revelation. But at the root of being a Puritan was an individual's experience of conversion. Puritan preaching and teaching were designed to call out not only rigid self-discipline, painstaking examination of conscience, and a sense of wickedness, but also the profound awareness of amazing grace, which made the elect person a saint.

When the effort to build the New Zion failed in Old England and New England, and the saints' children did not always see the light, Puritan values still created a tradition. It produced religious revivals, both as an individual search for salvation and for the social gospel, and it also helped develop the archetypal American character.

The true Puritan was self-reliant, self-governing, self-disciplining, and God-fearing. He had a limited sense of humor and, although greatly interested in education, he regarded the arts as "trimmings" and contributed little to them except biography and sermons. He distrusted big government but made "class peace" because Puritanism was a force that cut across social classes. He was honest, sober, responsible, and hard-working, qualities that made him a useful citizen and often a successful businessman.

Eliot shared many of those traits; others, not at all. In 1928 when he had just become both a British subject and member of the Church of England, Eliot wrote to an English friend that one day he wanted to write about "an American who wasn't an American," and belonged nowhere. He then described himself as born in the South, but sent to school in the East with a "nigger drawl." But at home he was not really a southerner because his family were northerners in a border state.

Eliot told his friend, Herbert Read, he had come to feel more French than American, then more English than French, but still felt that up to a hundred years ago, the whole United States had been his extended "family." Eliot added that to write such a story might be too difficult even for H. J. (Henry James), who had never had that kind of American roots.

It is doubtful if Eliot's statement made much sense to Read, but an American need not be an Eliot to understand Eliot's sense of dislocation. He had grown up in the Middle West in a city once led by his family, whose cultural and abolitionist politics had been swallowed up by more recent immigrants. Then he discovered that his family's Puritan heritage meant more to him than it did to the snobbish easterners with whom he went to school, so that, raised with a social conscience but no orthodox Christian dogmas, Eliot's idea of America seemed like a myth. For such an American, first Europe, then England, would be the obvious destination to recover his memory of things past, while providing a good vantage point from which to survey what was left of his native land.

As an answer to this dilemma Eliot helped to trail-blaze an American literary trend. Instead of the "romanticism" of pioneering, Eliot chose the "classicism" of reclaiming his traditions. Instead of cleaning up muckraked cities and ward politics, he chose to conquer the hierarchical society of a very class-conscious country. Instead of preaching the social gospel, he chose to proclaim orthodox Christianity. What Eliot, the displaced person, did not recognize for many years was that he approached all three in an American way, convinced that one's roots were crucial to the search for meaning.

Eliot came to share G. K. Chesterton's devotion to the idea of Christendom, or the Augustinian City of God to which C. S. Lewis, Charles Williams, and Dorothy L. Sayers paid allegiance. But Eliot also remained committed to his Puritan legacy, which demanded that he seek his own salvation, as well as follow the Puritan work ethic and civic-mindedness.

By the time T. S. Eliot was born in 1888, the Eliots, like many prosperous and famous New England families, knew a great deal about their early American ancestors, but less about their English antecedents. On his father's side, Eliot's forefathers had lived in southern England for several generations before immigrating to New England. One distinguished English relative was Sir Thomas Elyot, who sternly reproved Henry VIII to his face for consorting with Anne Boleyn. Sir Thomas also wrote a book on monarchy in which he scolded kings for their love of luxury and appealed to them to govern for the common good. Eliot was to quote Sir Thomas on marriage in his poem "East Coker."

His American ancestor, Andrew Eliot, a cordwainer, immigrated from East Coker to Beverly, Massachusetts, about 1669. According to family tradition, he then moved from Beverly to Salem, where he was a juror in the famous witch trials where Nathaniel Hawthorne's ancestor was a judge. Andrew Eliot later publicly repented his role, but the memory of witch-hanging remained in his family. As Eliot noted in his talk, "American Literature and the American Language," at St. Louis in 1953, there is something in Hawthorne's work that can best be appreciated by a reader with "Calvinism in his bones" and "witch-hanging on his conscience." There is a similar suggestion of blood guilt and the dark side of the American heritage in southerner William Faulkner's guilty relationship to his slave-owning ancestors. Both writers portrayed this "curse" as acting both communally and individually.

Like most Puritans the Eliot family did not come from a "steerage" class of immigrants: indentured servants, debtors, or political prisoners. They had done well enough in England to make wills, educate their sons, and occasionally marry into the landed gentry. They came to America with the Protestant conviction that every man, reading his Bible, was his own theologian, but they still regarded a Christian society as the proper source of authority.

The Eliot family became well known in Massachusetts as merchants, ministers, and educators. Staid and prosperous, the Eliots had a reputation for being serious moral men, not given to wild words and revolution. Andrew Eliot had not come to New England until the Restoration, so, presumably, he had found life under Oliver Cromwell satisfactory.

In America, one Eliot preacher lectured the colonial governor of Massachusetts in 1765 and kept his church open every Lord's Day during the British blockade. Another ancestor had his Boston house sacked by the British. William Greenleaf, sheriff of Boston in 1776, for whom Eliot's grandfather was named, defiantly read the Declaration of Independence from the balcony of the State House. Eliot's grandfather remembered the British bombardment of Baltimore in 1812, which gave birth to "The Star Spangled Banner." Those were the kinds of family memories that characterized the cultural inheritance of an American WASP (White Anglo-Saxon Protestant). For a WASP, the history of the country was an extension of family stories. After several centuries of use, its standards of behavior were almost genetically transmitted.

Eliot was raised with a serious, moral attitude toward living that was so bred in the bone that it became less a sense of good and evil than a sense of "what is and is not done." Years later Eliot told a young American friend that having given up smoking, he found it hard to eat candy because he had been raised not to indulge himself. Eliot was always regarded by his English friends as cautious and frugal in his own affairs, but generous in giving his time and resources to others.

By the late nineteenth century Eliot's family had published a genealogy, complete with family motto, *Tace et fac*, which may be translated "Be silent and get to work." It included some putative Norman ancestors, as well as collateral connections with the American presidential families of the Adamses and Rutherford Hayes.

On his mother's side Eliot could trace his family back to the beginning of New England and a wilder strain of missionary zeal. His mother's family, the Stearns, had arrived with John Winthrop in 1630 to build the New Jerusalem in Massachusetts Bay Colony before the Civil War began in England. It was primarily these earlier American settlers who were building the kingdom of God in a particular time and place.

Eliot's mother was a major influence on his choice of a literary career, but she also instilled in him an undying pride in his ancestors and a strong sense of their values. She herself was deeply interested in the characteristic Puritan search for salvation along with being public-spirited.

To be a WASP in America today is to be someone who is both enemy and target. But to describe Eliot as an American aristocrat is misleading.

American society has never been static enough to establish a permanent European class structure, only regional and ethnic cliques. Eliot's background has similarities with that of Henry James and Henry Adams, but to be an Eliot carries weight only in certain small circles, and in the popular mind is nothing at all like being a Rockefeller or even a Kennedy, true American plutocrats, born since Mark Twain's Gilded Age.

Ironically, critics also scold Eliot for being "off key" as an Englishman. They are unable to see that in many ways Eliot was a very good Englishman—of the seventeenth century. For a New England Eliot, there was always a sense in which the English Civil War had not yet ended, just as for Faulkner the American Civil War was not yet lost.

Unlike James or Adams, however, there was a second major strand in Eliot's American background: the Middle West. Eliot's birthplace was St. Louis, a bustling city perched by the Mississippi at the beginning of the "Wild West" of the American frontier. In "American Literature and the American Language," Eliot told his audience he was "very well satisfied" with having been born in St. Louis instead of Boston, New York, or London.

By American standards, St. Louis was an old city with a past as long as Boston's. Founded by French explorers in the seventeenth century, it was a center of prosperous fur trade with the Indians. During the nineteenth century St. Louis became a cosmopolitan American city, where some of the original French Roman Catholic settlers still lived. They were joined after the Revolutionary War by New England and southern pioneers moving west, and by a great wave of cultured, beer-drinking German immigrants.

Although Missouri was a border state with strong Southern sympathies, St. Louis was preserved for the Northern side in the Civil War, and was strategically important to General Grant's success in the West. As a growing city with important water and rail connections and a thriving cattle market, it was only gradually in the late nineteenth century that St. Louis lost out to Chicago as the chief center of the Middle West. Even then, Civil War veterans who followed Chicago's growing stockyards industry north raised their families with the image of a St. Louis that was far more civilized than raw, windblown Chicago.

In his lecture, Eliot was acknowledging in retrospect how much his work owed to his Middle Western origins and its images. His idea of culture was localized and particular, with a civilization rooted in time and place, and he came to see that St. Louis had filled that meaning in his life.

In common with Emerson and many other New Englanders, by the nineteenth century the Eliots had become Unitarians. They gave up their orthodox Congregationalism in favor of an understanding of God as apprehended by an "inner light," often combined with a messianic devotion to social action.

The most important part of Eliot's family code came from the Puritan "law of public service," which meant working for "Religion, Community, and Education." In St. Louis, those three institutions were represented for the Eliots by the Unitarian Church, the city, and Washington University. Two of the three owed their existence to Eliot's grandfather, William Greenleaf Eliot.

Eliot never knew him personally; his grandfather had died the year before his grandson was born. But, as Eliot told a Washington University audience, this frail man with the shining eyes, whom Ralph Waldo Emerson called the "Saint of the West," was still head of the family. Like Moses, his grandfather had brought down the family's own version of the tables of the law, from which "any deviation would be sinful." In retrospect, Eliot himself can be summed up as an equally frail but equally indomitable spokesman for religion, culture, and education.

William Greenleaf Eliot had come to the frontier in 1834 from Harvard Divinity School, where friends had felt "rebuked in his presence" because of his overwhelming spiritual devotion and inhuman drive. His dream was not to "convert" old Catholic St. Louis but to "civilize" it, to make it more like Unitarian Boston. St. Louis then was still a rough little river town, conscious of its French fur-trading origins, in spite of its recent German immigration and the railroads which had arrived to open up the West.

Within two years of his arrival Dr. Eliot had organized and built the thriving Unitarian Church of the Messiah. He tirelessly visited the sick, poor, prisoners, and inmates of mental asylums. When there was a cholera epidemic in 1849, Dr. Eliot worked around the clock.

He served as head of the city school board which made St. Louis one of the best systems in the country for its time; then he helped found a seminary which became Washington Institute, later Washington

University, as well as two secondary schools, Smith Academy and the Mary Institute. He taught at Washington and served as its third chancellor, but he refused to have the university named in his honor.

In the 1840s Missouri was a slave state and Dr. Eliot was passionately against slavery. But, like his deliberate and cautious grandson, the older man thought carefully before speaking out publicly against slavery or engaging in abolitionist demonstrations. Dr. Eliot knew that such extreme behavior would divide his flourishing church and city. Still, he was tempted to be a martyr to the cause, knowing his eastern friends would find him another pulpit and believing, too, that the "blood of the martyrs is the seed not only of the Church but of truth and liberty."

Dr. Eliot finally chose to work toward a general change of heart, hoping to effect change without confrontation. At the same time, whenever and wherever possible, he used the legal system to defend or protect individual slaves from harm. But when the Civil War broke out, Dr. Eliot was so upset at the idea of the nation itself breaking up that he spoke out publicly against slavery. Then he rallied the New Englanders and the Germans, who were strongly for the Union, with the result that St. Louis held for the North and became a vital key to winning the war.

Knowing that this was a war between brothers, Dr. Eliot was also concerned about prisons and prisoners. He organized the Western Sanitation Commission which provided services for both sides. He also handled his regular parish duties during the war and taught without pay at the new university.

He intervened in the case of Archer Alexander, a runaway slave who had saved a Union company from attack by walking through the night to warn them. Archer Alexander had escaped from his Mississippi owner and fled north to the Eliots in St. Louis. They offered to pay the owner his fair price. Instead the owner kidnapped Alexander, but Dr. Eliot got the local authorities to get him back, paid for his freedom, saw him freed, and then employed him until he died. Traveling after the war in Italy, Dr. Eliot saw the design for the Lincoln Memorial and arranged for Archer Alexander to be the model for the slave who kneels before Lincoln, breaking off his chains.

Dr. Eliot's Unitarianism was solid and conservative for such a liberal church. His Unitarian belief in human perfectibility was tempered by the idea that it was a slow process not easily achieved. He liked to emphasize the beliefs his church shared with other Christian churches and wished to preserve the past, however flawed. He also "loved the institutions of baptism and the Lord's Supper" and said that the communion table was the center of a church's religious life.

The story of this superman was not only common family lore and local history; his life was also written up in 1904 by Eliot's mother for her children "lest they forget." None of them could forget their grandfather. Rather, their main problem was how to emulate the family hero acceptably. Eliot himself, with his usual self-deprecating humor, told Washington University students that he blamed his grandfather's example for an "uncomfortable and very inconvenient obligation to serve on committees."

The story of Eliot's grandfather also helps explain why Eliot never completely subscribed to prevailing literary fashions. Writers like Virginia Woolf dismissed the older generation not so much for their beliefs as for their tendency to make readers feel that they must do something else—as if their writing were not a work of art complete in itself. Eliot was to be a spokesman for literature and an artist deeply interested in the craft of writing, but he never lost the sense of a moral purpose informing art.

Eliot, like Chesterton, did not find his grandfather's Unitarianism sufficient for his own spiritual needs. But speaking in St. Louis at the centennial of Washington University, he told his audience that he thought it a very good beginning for a child to be brought up to revere religion, the community, and education, and to subordinate personal and selfish aims to the general good.

CHAPTER TWO

Midwestern Boy
1888 – 1906

*I*N *Four Quartets*, ELIOT WAS TO SAY THAT "HOME IS WHERE ONE starts from," which is a far cry from his contemporary Robert Frost's comment that "Home is the place where, when you have to go there, they have to take you in." Eliot, on the contrary, spent his life seeking to understand his own roots in a personal parable of modern man's search for meaning. Although he rebelled from his family's expectations in many ways, at heart Eliot remained, and knew he remained, a typical representative of a remarkable tribe.

His quest was to lead him east, then back to England where he was finally buried in East Coker, the Somerset town from which his Eliot ancestor emigrated 300 years earlier. Eliot chose to end there, at his beginnings, because the village and church at East Coker still looked much the way it did in 1669, as well as through loyalty to his English citizenship and English wife. But the second line (from "Burnt Norton") inscribed on his grave pointed back across the Atlantic by saying, "In my end is my beginning."

When Thomas Stearns Eliot was born in 1888, although by American standards St. Louis was an old city, it still had a strong flavor of the frontier. As a child Eliot had thought "the Wild West" began at the end of the tram lines on Forest Park. He had grown up on stories of his father as a boy, spying on Indian encampments beyond the borders of the town, teasing the Indians with war whoops until chased back to town. Eliot probably also heard accounts of Indian uprisings and forced relocations, both of which were still occurring in the Middle West after the Civil War.

More important to young Tom Eliot was the fact that St. Louis owed its existence to the "long dark Mississippi." In his poem "The Dry Salvages," Eliot addressed the Mississippi as a "strong brown god—sullen, untamed and intractable," who had once been the mighty frontier, then became nothing but a problem for the builder of bridges. Unhonored and unpropitiated, the river continued to wait and watch, keeping its seasons and rages, a reminder of things people chose to forget.

Later, in his preface to Mark Twain's Mississippi River classic, *Huckleberry Finn*, which Eliot's strait-laced mother had not let him read as a boy, Eliot noted that its structure was built on the image of the river. He added that there was something about living beside a great river that cannot be explained to those who have not. As both a northerner and "New Englander by background" who had lived abroad, Eliot still felt that life in Missouri along the Mississippi had made a deeper impression on him.

In "The Dry Salvages" Eliot also recalled smelling the ailanthus trees by the river banks, climbing the limestone caves in search of fossils, and seeing the red cardinals flying overhead. Together with the Atlantic shores of New England, the Mississippi was to be Eliot's most powerful "family" image of time and eternity, as well as of the natural order that neither man nor machinery can quite control.

St. Louis also gave Eliot a strong sense of local particularity and urban loyalty. As a third-generation Middle Westerner, Eliot was an "old settler," and he grew up aware that his family was part of the governing group that gave St. Louis a culture of its own. Eliot always considered himself an urban poet; the city in his mind's eye was as much St. Louis as it was Boston, Paris, or London.

In the 1880s St. Louis was on the downhill path into political graft and corruption typical of many large industrial American cities. By 1902, when Tom Eliot was an impressionable teenager, Lincoln Steffens, a muckraker or investigative reporter, wrote an exposé of St. Louis for a *McClure's Magazine* series, *The Shame of the Cities*.

By the 1940s the original French town had been torn down, leaving the cathedral standing by itself in rubble. In 1948 Eliot wrote that modern civilization was destroying its ancient buildings to make a campsite for future barbarians. He was speaking about bomb-damaged London, but the same thing was true of his American hometown. When Eliot returned as a famous son in the early '50s, the city he knew was nearly gone, destroyed by waves of slum and land clearance.

His grandfather's Church of the Messiah was on Locust Street, not far from the large, comfortable frame house where Eliot grew up. As an infant, Thomas Stearns Eliot was baptized there. The St. Louis Eliots were raised in Unitarianism's ethical humanism, which demanded public service, thrift, and moral optimism. Eliot's family stressed a Quakerish "high thinking and plain living." The Puritan preoccupation with heaven and hell and the salvation of one's soul was passed over in favor of preaching the social gospel. Although Unitarianism was increasingly syncretistic in its use of texts by oriental and Indian philosophers, it was not much interested in the private, introspective life of contemplation, although one Eliot cousin did become a Buddhist.

A generation earlier English apologist G. K. Chesterton had been raised in a surprisingly similar, middle-class home in Kensington, London. There Chesterton also learned local loyalty and later, like Eliot, he paid tribute to his family's high standards of business ethics and civic responsibility. Chesterton's parents had also believed in the fatherhood of God, the brotherhood of man, and the inevitability of progress, and took their sons to hear a flamboyant Unitarian minister who preached Fabian socialism. Then, just as Eliot was to do, Chesterton shocked his parents by "turning back" to the orthodox Christian roots of their liberal creed.

Chesterton's quiet and humorous father had no wish to work at the family real estate business and quit as soon as he could afford to. Eliot's father, Henry Ware Eliot, did not do as his dynamic father wished and go into the Unitarian ministry. When told he had "wasted" his education, Eliot's father responded that "too much pudding had stuffed the dog."

Henry Eliot had wanted to be a painter, and it was he who filled the Eliot house with reproductions of famous paintings like Murillo's "Immaculate Conception," which young Tom remembered in his mother's bedroom. Eliot's father also appreciated the music for which St. Louis was famous. Finding an artistic career impractical in his family, Henry Ware Eliot became a successful businessman. When Tom was born he was president of the Hydraulic-Press Brick Company, well able to be philanthropic and sit on committees.

By then Eliot's father was in his late forties and was going deaf. He was remembered by his children as a quiet gentleman of charm and humor, given to teasing ("leg pulls") like his son, Tom. Tom Eliot's own correct, demure behavior hid not only a sly sense of humor, but also a lifelong, adolescent fondness for practical jokes. Eliot's father was a champion chess player who drew cat faces on his children's breakfast eggs.

Again like the Chesterton household, the dominant Eliot parent was his mother, Charlotte Champe Stearns. She was one of the kind of strong-minded American women bred by the Puritan and pioneer experience. Raised in the Boston area near Lexington she was an excellent student, but she was not allowed to follow her heart's desire and attend college. Instead, by age twenty she was earning her own living as a schoolteacher in St. Louis, where she met and married Eliot's father in 1868.

Charlotte Eliot saw to it that her daughters all attended college. It was her generation in America who became the backbone of the post Civil War suffragette movement and worked hard at civic affairs, in addition to running large households with many children and heavy social responsibilities.

Charlotte Eliot belonged to several clubs devoted to literature or civic improvements. These clubs raised funds for special projects like settlement houses, visited jails and hospitals, and ran the cultural subscription series that brought famous people to lecture. Charlotte's most impressive project was her work on behalf of juvenile delinquents, whom she did not want treated as a part of the adult justice system. She raised money for a probation officer, got a juvenile court established and a separate detention home built. Her family was proud of her work; her husband kept a scrapbook about her public recognition, and their oldest daughter Ada did similar work in New York City.

The real ambition of Charlotte Eliot's life, however, was to be a published poet. She passed along this ambition, together with a strong interest in the "inner light," to her younger son. She wrote poetry all her life, but was published only in religious magazines. Her poems were trite and didactic, sounding a lot like hymns. They usually dealt with religious or historical subjects, such as the Annunciation, the wise men, or St. Ambrose. Her epic poem about Savonarola, the puritanical monk who tried to reform Medici Florence and was burned at the stake, was finally published in 1926 through her son's efforts.

His mother pasted her published poems in a scrapbook, which with her notebooks, survives in the family papers. Eliot undoubtedly read or heard most of her poems as a boy. Although he wrote on similar subjects, how far his mother's poems "converted" his imagination is hard to judge; their poetical style is very different.

Like the Eliots, Charlotte Stearns came from Puritan stock, so her son inherited a double dose of their self-examining, self-doubting, highly critical ways. In such families, praise comes seldom, blame is inevitable, and moralizing is the order of the day. In 1904, as if to underline this attitude, Charlotte published her life of her father-in-law to remind her children to "make the best of every faculty and control every tendency to evil." Clearly, Charlotte Eliot was both preacher and teacher, characteristics her son displayed in his own career.

Like most middle-class American households at that time, the Eliots had several servants, including a housemaid, a gardener or handyman, and an Irish nursemaid (whose name was Annie Dunne) for Tom. Eliot remembered going with Annie to the Roman Catholic Church at Locust and Jefferson Street. There he was taken inside a "dark and holy place" where he saw colorful statues and tiny flickering lights, mixed with the smell of incense and wax and the sounds of chanting in a strange tongue. According to Eliot, he and Annie, of whom he was very fond, seriously discussed the proofs of the existence of God when he was only six. Her everyday Catholic practices must have made a deep impression on him, too. He would have seen her missal and rosary, and perhaps known about the feast and fast days she observed.

There were seven Eliot children, six of whom lived. Eliot had four older sisters and one brother, Henry Ware Eliot, Junior, who was nine years his senior and to whom he was very close. Although described by an Eliot cousin as not very "motherly," Charlotte Eliot fussed over the baby, who was never robust. Because Eliot had been born with a congenital double hernia, his mother refused to let him roughhouse or play active team sports, which isolated him from other boys.

At home, unlike C. S. Lewis or G. K. Chesterton or Virginia Woolf, Eliot had no peer to be his friend and ally. At the same time, surrounded by his sisters, Eliot learned to appreciate the society of women as much as men, an American trait not often found in his English friends.

Like Dorothy Sayers, Eliot could always count on an admiring audience of older relatives. As a result, both later characterized themselves as "prigs," who learned to bury their heads in a book when they wanted privacy. Both Eliot and Sayers grew up to be shy, rather formal people whose public personas were always something of an "act." They behaved naturally only with close friends.

In one of Eliot's *Ariel* poems, "Animula," written in the '30s after he had become a Christian, he described a small child very like himself. The "simple soul" lurks about under tables and the chairs of grownups. He notices everything, runs toward and then away from kisses and toys. As he sits curled up in a window seat, hiding behind the *Encyclopaedia Britannica*, he is aware that life is both "what the fairies do and what the servants say." In his childhood pictures Eliot is chubby and cheerful-looking, with his mother's deep eyes.

Eliot's parents were both in their forties when he was born. Brought up in an adult household, he proved to be their most gifted child, as well as a precocious "only child." Once his mother realized that Tom was gifted she began to treat him as an equal. She encouraged him to develop an interest in literature, especially in the poet John Milton, a Puritan favorite; in Matthew Arnold, the English critic of culture; and in Ralph Waldo Emerson, the literary embodiment of Unitarianism. Like any normal child, Eliot grew up with a strong dislike for all three poets and became famous for criticizing their works.

On the other hand, his family's celebration of Christmas made a lifelong impression on him, to which, like Chesterton, he ascribed a holy awe that helped bring him to Christianity. In "Animula" Eliot described the fragrant brilliance of a Christmas tree. Then, in "The

Cultivation of Christmas Trees," he praised the child's sense of wonder at the Christmas feast as the beginning of a great joy, which is also a great fear because the first coming reminds us of the second.

Eliot said that he had been happiest during his childhood and the last years of his life, after he had remarried, and he retained an affection for children. Many years later his young cousin Teddy Welch was taken to visit Eliot's cousin Eleanor Hinkley, who had never married but lived with her widowed mother in Cambridge, Massachusetts. Bored by the grownups, Teddy went into the dining room and hid under the table, covered with a lace tablecloth. There he was discovered by his cousin Tom, who was also visiting from England. Eliot had sent Teddy an autographed copy of *Old Possum's Book of Practical Cats*, so Teddy asked Eliot to recite "The Song of the Jellicles." To do so properly, Eliot joined Teddy under the dining room table, where they were both discovered by the other adults.

Eliot first went to Miss Lockwood's primary school on Vanderventer Place, where he rapidly became a scholastic star, completing his lessons faster and better than anyone else in his class. At the same time, as if anticipating his future career as editor and critic, Eliot published for his adoring family a "little paper" called "The Fireside." It contained "Fiction, Gossip and Theatre," all written by "Thos. S. Eliot." As editor of "The Fireside," Eliot also wrote and illustrated "George Washington, A Life, 1st Ed."

Much later, however, when Eliot submitted poems to a family newspaper written by his Morley godchildren, none of his poems about cats was accepted. The Morley children's father, American Frank Morley, was a close friend of Eliot's, who worked with him at Faber & Faber and also on *The Criterion* until he and his family returned to America.

Another family memento from Eliot's childhood was a large copy of *Don Quixote*, illustrated by Gustave Dore. It had belonged to Eliot's father who had called it "The Donkey Book," and it was sat on by young Eliots at family celebrations like Christmas and Thanksgiving. In 1930 when their father had died, Eliot's brother Henry inscribed it "For Tom—from his brother Henry, 1930" and sent it off to London. Eliot pasted his elephant bookplate in the book, and faithfully lugged it with him until 1936, when he gave it to the Morley family with an additional inscription of his own. Morley ownership of "The Donkey

Book" meant that Eliot's family treated the Morleys as family. After Eliot's death, Frank Morley described himself as having played Sancho Panza to Eliot's Don Quixote.

In 1898, when he was ten, Eliot was sent to Smith Academy, founded by his grandfather. It was a private preparatory school for Washington University. Its sister school, the Mary Institute, was next door to his own house, separated by a locked gate and a garden wall. As a boy Eliot remembered hearing the voices of children playing there. Once he discovered the key and unlocked the door in the wall to explore while the girls were not there. The imagery of this adventure was to become part of "Burnt Norton."

When he came back to St. Louis in 1953 Eliot took pleasure in reciting the names of his teachers at Smith Academy and said he had received the most important part of his education there. Eliot took Latin and Greek, together with Greek and Roman history, English and American history, elementary mathematics, French, German, and English. It was a typical American college preparatory course for the period, more classical than the ordinary high-school curriculum, but much less narrowly classical than an English public school. It gave students a basis for understanding their own culture and language, as well as that of modern Europe. Here and at Harvard, Eliot was educated to be an American, not an Englishman, and he never lost that breadth of cultural outlook.

While he was at Smith, Eliot also began his public career as a poet. He said he first had a natural, boyish enthusiasm for "martial and sanguinary poetry" like Macaulay's "How Horatius Kept the Bridge," which belonged with pea shooters and lead soldiers. Then from twelve to fourteen he was not much interested in poetry until, in what Sayers called the "dreamy, poetic stage," he picked up Fitzgerald's translation of the *Rubaiyat of Omar Khayyam*. Eliot was transfixed by its new world painted in bright and painful colors and tried writing some gloomy quatrains which he destroyed. Then he embarked on a normal adolescent poet's course, reading Byron, Keats, and Shelley, together with Swinburne and Rossetti.

Eliot recalled that Mr. Hatch, the Smith English teacher, commended the first poem he submitted, although he also asked if Eliot had any help with it. Eliot's first public reading was at his Smith graduation in 1905, where he read the valedictory poem. He dryly added that his teacher told him that the poem was good, but his delivery was not. The Smith Academy valedictory poem was later published in the *Harvard Advocate*.

In his future poetic career, along with the Mississippi River and St. Louis, the other landscape that influenced Eliot was the coast of New England and the Atlantic Ocean. St. Louis was hot and steamy in summer, and most middle-class families fled to the cool lakes of the north. The Eliots, however, spent their summers on the east coast, where they had many relatives.

From 1893, when Eliot was only five, they went every summer by train to Gloucester, Massachusetts. Then in 1896 his father built a house called Eastern Point near Gloucester on the Atlantic coast, looking out to the dangerous, half-submerged rocks called the Dry Salvages. This house, which remained in his family, gave a sense of permanence and roots to Eliot's adult visits home, keeping his New England memories green.

During those summers, young Eliot had moments of intense and lovely solitude that he always remembered, "unattended moments" that gave him a sense of the meaning of existence. He might gaze into a seaside pool and see a sea anemone or a horseshoe crab, hear the roar of the surf or the bell on the rocks in the bay. Those memories, recaptured in his poetry, were close to the "joy" with which young C. S. Lewis saw the tiny garden in his brother's hand.

In "The Influence of Landscape on A Poet," Eliot called himself a New England poet because the scenery there had made such a deep impression on him. After his death Eliot's friend and editor Robert Giroux wrote that Eliot was always happy near the sea. Even as a small boy, the ocean meant haven and calm to Eliot; it became an image of eternity for him. The fishermen's dangerous calling to follow the sea came to embody his quest for meaning. Sailors were explorers in whom he could see his own ancestors with similarly dour but heroic natures. Eliot's joy intensified when he was allowed to learn to sail; then he could escape on the sea itself.

When he graduated from Smith Academy, instead of going to Washington University like his father and brother, Eliot was sent east to spend an extra year at Milton Academy. His parents planned to send him to Harvard University, but his mother felt that at seventeen he was still too young. She wrote the headmaster that she also hoped he would have a chance to enjoy friendships with boys his own age.

Considering the fact that eastern students tend to be a parochial, cliquish lot, she was probably wise. Coming from Milton Academy which had been founded in 1798 as a prep school for Harvard would help Eliot at Harvard, where his Eliot connections alone would not insure his social acceptance among his classmates. He also may have needed extra classes or coaching to get into Harvard, since he had taken virtually no science courses at Smith.

Eliot did make two friends that year, both of whom went on to Harvard with him. One was Howard Morris, with whom he roomed his sophomore year in college. The other was Scofield Thayer, who later was publisher of *The Dial*.

It may have been during his Milton year that his big brother Henry took Eliot to New York where they rode down Fifth Avenue in a hansom cab to see a George M. Cohan musical. Eliot's love affair with musicals, vaudeville, and song and dance lasted all his life. According to Roger Giroux, in the 1950s Eliot could still sing all the songs George M. Cohan ever wrote, and he had loved it when Eartha Kitt sang "T. S. Eliot writes pomes to me" in the review *New Faces*. Eliot promptly sent Kitt roses.

Not much more is known about his Milton year. His mother kept close track of his illnesses and activities by letter, while Eliot took courses like history, physics, and chemistry to pass the Harvard entrance exams. He also became self-conscious about his Missouri twang and tried to lose it. Outwardly his Milton year made Eliot an acceptable easterner, but inwardly it did not really "take."

In 1933, when he spoke to the Milton graduating class, Eliot evoked a rather sad ghost of his seventeen-year-old self. But his remarks, addressed to his former self, were probably the result of having just left his wife Vivien for good, rather than memories of the school.

Eliot remembered himself as an indecisive young man, always four or five experiments behind in science. He wished now that he could tell himself "what a mess he had made of things."

Then he gave the Milton boys some very stoic advice. They should not admire or hope for success, because it would feel just the same as failure. Instead, they should discover the right thing to do and then do it. But whatever action they took, no matter what happened, they should not complain but take the consequences. Finally, Eliot told the Milton graduates that they should not think, or want, or feel the way their parents or peers wanted them to. Instead, they must try to be emotionally honest with themselves. He added that they must do it, no matter how hard it was.

CHAPTER THREE

Easterner
1906 – 1914

*T*OM ELIOT ENTERED HARVARD UNIVERSITY ON HIS EIGHTEENTH birthday, September 26, 1906. He took his B.A. in 1909, his master's in 1910, and, after a year in Paris, returned in 1911 to spend three more years at Harvard, teaching and working on his Ph.D. in philosophy. Outwardly he was a budding academic being groomed to reestablish the importance of his branch of the Eliot family in the home of its American roots.

After a year at Milton Academy young Eliot presumably understood that if you go east to stay you must appear "more eastern than the easterners," joining them in their inability to locate places like Omaha, Nebraska, or Chicago, Illinois. But Eliot never lost his sense of the West nor the world outside Boston. In a poem written in French during one of his "dry spells," he called himself a "professor in America, a journalist in England," never at home anywhere in the world "from Damascus to Omaha."

But it is difficult to determine just what effect Harvard and Boston had on Eliot. Outwardly he played the role of the proper student to perfection. What is not so clear is which influenced Eliot more: his self-education or the eastern ambiance. Eliot never looked like a rebel; he said that he did not act unconventional because he felt so unconventional inside. But most critics cling to the romantic idea that revolutions must be started by bohemian-looking types who defy social instead of literary conventions.

At the time Eliot went there, Harvard University was experiencing a "golden era." There were many famous names on the faculty. The university was having a period of great growth and expansion, during which the student body became much larger and more diversified, and many buildings were added. Although Henry Adams complained that its intellectual atmosphere was "cold and unsociable," Harvard's elective system was very American by contrast with the structure of an English university, where a student read one subject like classics or history for three years.

A distant Eliot cousin, Charles W. Eliot, was president, presiding over a faculty of luminaries like William James, James Russell Lowell, George Santayana, Josiah Royce, the disaffected Henry Adams, and Charles Copeland, as well as one professor of whom young T. S. Eliot spoke highly, Irving Babbitt. There was also an occasional distinguished visitor like English philosopher Bertrand Russell.

President Eliot's elective system fostered breadth at the expense of depth. He thought that all the humanities an American needed to know were contained in his famous fifty-volume Harvard Classics. This famous "Five Foot Shelf" was not intended, like the Great Books curriculum of President Robert Hutchins of the University of Chicago, to provide a thorough understanding of civilization, but to fill in the cultural gaps in the education of working men and women.

As a student at Harvard, Eliot was also introduced to "Brahmin" Back Bay society, a genteel and parochial milieu. His uncle, Christopher Eliot, was a prominent local Unitarian minister, so Eliot's place at tea dances and membership in the right clubs was assured.

That tight little world had been made famous by an earlier expatriate, Henry James, and had been rebelled against by Henry Adams, who was unreconciled to his family's loss of national power and prestige. Like Eliot, both came from old New England stock, but such ancestry counted for less and less in an industrial country run by steel and railway magnates and ethnic politicians.

Eliot found this society empty, although he politely went through the proper gestures. His real reactions appeared in his first Modernist poems, published in *Prufrock and Other Observations 1917*. They show Eliot's sardonic eye for the foibles he observed in his relations and other proper Bostonians. "Cousin Nancy" was a would-be modern who danced the new dances and smoked, against the advice of her aunts and their twin authorities, "Matthew" (Arnold) and "Waldo" (Emerson). "Aunt Helen" was a maiden lady who lived a self-centered life in which her pet dogs and Dresden clock were her most important possessions. Both were the subjects of poems in *Prufrock*. In another poem, *The Boston Evening Transcript* was Cousin Harriet's substitute for real life.

Apart from "The Love Song of J. Alfred Prufrock," the most famous of these poems was his Jamesian "Portrait of a Lady." This poem was a description of a would-be Madame de Stael with a salon of callow college boys. Eliot's friend Conrad Aiken remarked that in this poem Eliot had pinned Miss X like a butterfly to the page.

Whether or not as a sheltered adolescent Eliot had been aware of the growing corruption and vulgarity of St. Louis, he explored Boston beyond Beacon Hill. The many urban images in his poetry owe as much to prewar Boston as postwar London. "Preludes," his grim glimpse of the city as the nadir of civilization, was based on the Boston slums of Roxbury and Charleston. The poem makes an interesting contrast to the beatific image of the city as the citadel of Christendom, about which Eliot's friend, English poet Charles Williams, wrote. The young Eliot came closer to the true Augustinian model, with its contrast between the two cities—temporal and eternal.

Eliot's urban explorations represented a moral and physical enterprise impressive in someone raised as he was. They may reflect his family's social-service orientation, but they were also an effort to outgrow their protection and observe reality for himself.

Most of Eliot's time, however, was taken up with his studies. Having lost the religious convictions (if any) of his childhood, Eliot was still motivated by the family's sense of duty, which led him to pursue his education with ferocious thoroughness.

Harvard undergraduate Conrad Aiken described his shy friend Eliot as "singularly attractive, tall and rather dapper." Aiken nicknamed Eliot "the Tsetse" (fly)—one who was somewhat waspish in his pronouncements (like Aiken himself). Eliot's college photographs show a good-looking, slender, nattily dressed young undergraduate, who could easily become a London banker with a fedora, double-breasted dark suit, and furled umbrella, in dramatic contrast to the poetic image Eliot conveyed in verse.

As an undergraduate, Eliot was already known for being precise, even pedantic in his use of language. He corrected his fellow students' quotations, and, better read than most of them, he also told them what they meant. At the same time Eliot was typically far more of a listener and observer.

Only his intimate friends, then and later, knew him to be a friendly, witty person, who loved music halls, wrote bawdy verse, collected examples of slang, read comic strips, and loved to play elaborate practical jokes. Two characteristics that Eliot retained all his life, which critics found difficult to reconcile, were already evident in his undergraduate days: a Puritan conscience combined with a sense of humor. By the time he was an undergraduate, Eliot was already being accused of "playing a part" or, in Freudian jargon, of wearing a mask to disguise his feelings.

In the early twentieth century, Cambridge was still a small college town. Its elm-shaded village streets were lined with white picket fences and lilac bushes. Its boardwalks were put down in winter and taken up in summer, and the sound of the college bell "reverberated over all."

During his freshman year Eliot lived on Mount Auburn Street on Cambridge's "Gold Coast," not far from the home of the poet Longfellow. Those rooms no doubt were chosen by his mother since she still worried about his health. His second and third year, he roomed at Russell Hall with Howard Morris, a pudgy, unintellectual friend from Milton Academy. Their rooms were typical student quarters of the period, with comfortable Morris chairs, divan, oriental rug, magazines and books, fireplace, and tea things, lit with both gas jets and electricity. There were photographs of families and athletic teams and a Harvard banner on the wall.

Essentially a loner, Eliot made only a few friends outside his family

and its connections. Among those who visited his family at Cape Ann
and sailed with him to Canada was William Tinckom-Fernandez, who
was several years older. "Tinck" was expelled before graduation for
cutting classes, but he showed Eliot some of Ezra Pound's poetry before
he took off for Europe.

Another student named Harold Peters got Eliot interested in physical fitness. They went to a South Boston gym for workouts with an ex-
fighter, who may be the model for Eliot's Sweeney. Eliot also went
religiously to the theater and the Boston Symphony. Famous
classmates of Eliot's with whom he had little contact were the revolutionary John Reed (who is buried in Red Square), political commentator Walter Lippman, and economist Stuart Chase.

Eliot joined the Southern Club, but his membership had to be
negotiated because no one was sure if St. Louis *was* in the South, and
the Digamma. Later he joined the Signet and the Stylus, "writing"
clubs. The Signet and the *Harvard Advocate*, where he and Conrad
Aiken were editors in 1908-1909, gave him most of his literary friends.

In spite of his disapproval of the elective system, Eliot took advantage of it to choose what he needed or wanted. As an undergraduate
he continued with Latin and Greek, and added German, art,
philosophy, and history. He avoided math and science in which he did
poorly and had little interest.

Later, earning his living in London as a freelance "journalist," Eliot
fleshed out his essays and reviews with material from those Harvard
classes. He also chose for review books by his former professors such
as Charles Haskins's *The Renaissance of the Twelfth Century*.

Eliot's second year at Harvard was a watershed for his goals and ambition. He had decided to take his degree in three years, but he was not
greatly impressed by his professors. He had English under Professor
Copeland, who favored a journalistic style of writing and accused
young Eliot of being too precise. Nor was Eliot impressed by William
James's pragmatic philosophy of optimism because it made man the
measure of all things. He was also not convinced that George
Santayana's iconoclastic "Toryism" was much better.

On his own, Eliot had begun to study two of the three poets who
were to exercise important influences on his own development. The
three poets were Dante, Baudelaire, and Laforgue. In Eliot's last essay

on Dante, published in 1950, he told of his lasting debt to all three. He said that together they represented the poles of sensibility that encompassed his own cultural horizons and ambition.

For Eliot, Dante was the poet of a united Europe or Christendom. Dante had written in medieval Italian, which was the closest thing to a universal lingua franca with its close roots to medieval Latin; he brilliantly combined poetry and philosophy in a robe without a seam. As Eliot wrote in his first essay on Dante, published in 1920, philosophy cannot originate in poetry, but poetry can deal with philosophy, once it has reached the point of (cultural) acceptance.

Eliot's lifelong ambition was to be a philosopher poet like Dante, and both he and his critics categorize his mature poetry in Dantean terms. His poetic *Inferno* extended from *J. Alfred Prufrock* through *The Waste Land*. His *Purgatorio* was contained in *The Hollow Men* and *Ash Wednesday*. His *Paradiso* was *Four Quartets*.

Baudelaire was the first modern poet to write about the decay of Dantean civilization and to describe the horror and ugliness of cities. Baudelaire gave young Eliot the idea of the poetic possibilities of describing in English the sordid aspects of the cities he had seen, as well as fusing and juxtaposing that grim realism with fantastic visions. Baudelaire had an extremely self-conscious style and a highly morbid imagination, and he taught Eliot how to turn the unpoetical into poetry.

Finally, in Jules Laforgue, whom he read last, Eliot recognized a temperament akin to his own. Laforgue was an ironic dandy whose writings helped Eliot discover his own form and gave him a model with which to restructure his own work.

To anyone interested in the development of the mature Eliot, the most important of the three is Dante. In addition to the many Dantean echoes that appear in his poetry, Eliot wrote three pivotal essays about Dante. In the 1920 essay Eliot defended the possibility of a philosophic poet; in the second, he discussed the *Divine Comedy* as poetry; and in the last, he described how as a young Harvard sophomore he first met the real "il miglior fabbro" of his own career.

Paradoxically, Eliot was introduced to Dante about 1910 by the casual Harvard "system." He did not study Dante in class, but was encouraged to plunge into the *Divine Comedy*, reading the medieval Italian with the help of a prose translation, half understanding and half learning the language as he went along. Many years later, Dorothy L. Sayers followed the same route, reading the original and a prose translation side by side, and becoming so fascinated that she undertook a modern English translation.

Undergraduate Eliot steeped himself in Dante's poetry. When he had puzzled out the meaning of a canto that delighted him, he memorized it, so that he could recite it "lying in bed or taking the train." Dante's European world view, Christian beliefs, and Thomist philosophy became a part of the young Eliot. Dante exerted a continuing influence on the adult Eliot, pointing him toward his conversion and commitment to the idea of an orthodox Christian community.

Eliot met Conrad Aiken, a young, redheaded future poet in the spring of 1908 at a *Lampoon* party. As fellow editors of the *Harvard Advocate* they continued to meet, sharing an enthusiasm for slang, comic strips, and salacious verses like Eliot's unpublished ones about "King Bolo." Mostly they talked and talked about writing—what to write and how to write and where to write. Aiken was in favor of England; Eliot, like many an American before him, thought Paris the promised land.

Eliot's desire to escape abroad he called a case of "the old American malaise." In the *Harvard Advocate* he reviewed Van Wyck Brooks's first book on American literature, *The Wine of the Puritans*. In his review he described the dilemma of Americans like Henry James, whose hearts were in the Old Country but whose future and fortune lay in the New. Eliot also wrote an essay for the *Harvard Advocate* called "Gentlemen and Seamen." In it he praised the "plebeian aristocracy" of New England's sailors, finding in their faces his own forebears. Here Eliot was not talking as a self-ordained American "aristocrat"; the sailors or men like them were his ancestors, and he was extolling their exploring spirit.

Then in December 1908 Eliot ran across a book in the Harvard Union library which changed his life. It gave him a form in which to write his poetry and—to some extent—a way to act the part of poet. It also made him aware of the literary avant-garde's zeitgeist, the feeling in the air that Virginia Woolf was to call a "change in human nature." That spirit was brilliantly summed up by Yeats's poem "The Second Coming," in which he described the artist's despair at communicating to a world with a broken center.

The life-changing book was Arthur Symons's *The Symbolist Movement in Literature*. In it Symons called for art to become a religion to provide the poet and his audience an escape from time and mortality. Symons saw the artist as an Orpheus, a prophet of the unknown who would create a new world, helping society shed the bondage of the old. But to do so, every artist was forced to construct his own vision and be his own guide. In turn, this role made him acutely aware of modern man's sense of loneliness and alienation in a world where Nietzsche had declared that God is dead.

The writers who were to exemplify that Orphic role the best were Franz Kafka and James Joyce—and, in the pivotal role of modern spokesman and seer, but finally believer, T. S. Eliot. Despite their quarrel with romanticism, in Eliot's case with Arnold and Emerson, these writers were all its direct heirs, bent on improvising a shape and significance to experience that would make it useful for art.

During the early twentieth century most major English writers like Joyce, Shaw, Yeats, Lawrence, Henry James, Joseph Conrad, and even E. M. Forster and Virginia Woolf, were working within this aesthetic. These writers rejected Christianity but used it for their primary metaphors, accepting Easter, for example, as a folk ritual. Instead of being Christians, these writers were religious about life, where they caught glimpses of reality in moments of self-identity, or "epiphanies." They created meaning in their works by using a thematic unity, often ancient myths, and kept their characters under tight control, having no use for "heroic" heroes. From these Symbolists came the Imagist poets, who worked to obtain a "classic" impersonality and objectivity. They led to the Vorticist movement, which called for the artist to disappear into his work, becoming the "invisible poet."

Thanks to Symons, it was the French poets who were directly responsible for Eliot's introduction to this aesthetic and to a new verse form that allowed him to express his fragmented experiences and emotions. Symons did this by quoting extensively from the works of late nineteenth-century French poets like Baudelaire, Verlaine, Rimbaud, and the less well-known Jules Laforgue.

Eliot later described Laforgue as a "smaller poet," who directed his first steps "like an admired elder brother." Reading the samples of

Laforgue quoted by Symons, Eliot was so taken by his work that he went to a foreign bookshop in Boston and ordered all of Laforgue's poetry. Laforgue wrote with dry, deliberate irony and liked to disguise his own voice by playing different roles. By using these personae, Laforgue dramatized his serious ideas as ridiculous or irrational feelings. In person, Laforgue was a dapper Edwardian dandy, a pose Eliot had learned at Harvard and felt comfortable with.

Eliot received his copy of Laforgue's poems by late spring 1909. He received his B.A. that June. Neither he nor war poet Alan Seeger was elected Class Poet, but Eliot was chosen Class Odist and wrote a conventional verse to "Fair Harvard," which gave no hint of J. Alfred Prufrocks to come. After graduation Eliot spent the summer of 1909 at Cape Ann with his family. There with Laforgue's help he set to work to do what Ezra Pound later called "modernizing himself on his own."

Most of the poems Eliot was working on, like "Conversation Galante," "Nocturne," and "Humoresque," were modeled directly after his French sources. They first appeared in a notebook found in the Berg Collection at New York's Public Library. Eliot had purchased the notebook in summer 1910, calling it "The Complete Poems of T. S. Eliot." Later he added the ironic subtitle, "Inventions of the March Hare."

Eliot copied all his "new" poems into this notebook. Some of them were later published in *Prufrock*, others in *Poems Written in Early Youth*. A number have never been published at all, but have been used by critics to guess at Eliot's state of mind (Eliot typically dated his work in progress). Eliot continued to add to this notebook until he went to England in 1914; it provides a kind of diary of this transitional period in his life.

The poems demonstrate Eliot's growing wish to get away from the pressures of family expectations and of academia itself, as well as from the genteel society of Boston, which stood for modern America. The poems also show Eliot's search for a sense of what he called "the Absolute," or a sense of reality and meaning to be met in moments outside time. That was the appropriate route for any apprentice Orpheus, but for Eliot there was also another dimension. From late adolescence Eliot's solitary sense of sin and guilt (mere baggage from the past to other young rebels) meant that, like C. S. Lewis seeking more glimpses of "Joy," the visions Eliot did receive were a kind of torment. They suggested a whole experience just beyond his reach. Neither Eliot nor Lewis was willing to settle for mere moments of illumination.

Eliot returned to Harvard the fall of 1910 to work on his M.A. in English literature. He studied very hard, perhaps to earn the right to take off on his own, and lived by himself at Apley Court, avoiding his friends. That November he wrote another group of "new" poems. About January 1911 he wrote one called "Spleen," in which a middle-aged gentleman's manners kept him from getting past the "doorstep" of "the Absolute."

Many of his notebook poems described Eliot's wish to get away from his studies, as well as from his family's demand that he decide what he was going to do. Eliot also wrote about escaping from women, not just from "sirens," but also from his bossy, ever-anxious mother and sisters. His wish to escape was bound up with his determination to go to Paris.

Prewar Paris, of course, was a dream city for Eliot. He believed that there he could become a poet without criticism, and could take part in some great salon of art and conversation. He dreamed of sampling a heady mixture of the cultivated European life described by Henry James and *la vie boheme*. But his family, especially his mother, felt that if Eliot wished to be a writer, he should live in New York. France seemed dangerously foreign, a place to visit as a tourist and then return safely home.

While he worked on his new poems and his master's degree Eliot took a course in French literature from Irving Babbitt. Babbitt was an important influence on Eliot's philosophy, although he and Eliot eventually fell out over Eliot's "backsliding" to Christianity.

Babbitt was an outspoken apostle of humanism. He believed that man was a higher order of creation but must work to develop his own higher nature. That nature derived from respect for the wisdom of one's ancestors and apprehension of the nature of good and evil. For Babbitt the arts were a discipline designed to teach man to control his will and appetites. The American cult of progress and egalitarian education were anathema to him; he stood for standards, discipline, order. Because Babbitt was also well read in Indian philosophy, his class probably gave Eliot the interest in Eastern studies which he pursued in graduate school.

In an essay written ten years later, Eliot talked about the parasitical relationship between Babbitt's humanism and Christianity. Historically, humanism depended on the Christian tradition for its existence. By appealing to the individual's use of "inner checks" to keep society functioning, Babbitt was trying to "build a Catholic platform out of Protestant planks."

Like many of the great writers of the period, Babbitt seemed to end in a "Catholicism of despair," in which he felt that the Roman Catholic Church might be preferable to Bolshevism. Eliot dryly noted that a study of Roman Catholic history might strike one with awe, but not tempt one to place all the hopes of humanity in that one institution. He concluded that Babbitt knew too much about too many religions to be able to believe in any.

Meanwhile, Eliot's own poems show him engaged in a typical intelligent and sensitive adolescent's soul-searching. Much of his agonizing reflected, too, a late sexual development that terrified him. At the same age G. K. Chesterton was confiding to his notebooks both his solipsistic fears about a meaningless world where he could not see his own role and his belatedly awakened terrors about sex, violence, and women. Chesterton later wrote many stories about similar young men, but at the time was able to share some of them with his friend Bentley. Eliot seems to have had no one; his friend Conrad Aiken had already embarked on a pattern of casual sex repugnant to anyone raised as Eliot had been. Unlike C. S. Lewis, who was writing his woes to Arthur Greeves, neither Chesterton nor Eliot felt comfortable settling down into an academic career which the parents of both would have accepted.

Compared to either Chesterton or Lewis, however, Eliot's descriptions of these existential problems have a bias toward asceticism and martyrdom, or what mystics called the Negative Way, which was to reappear in his later work. Those ideas may be a legacy of his mother's spiritual yearnings, but Eliot did not express them in her conventional images or language, nor did he share her essentially optimistic nature. Although a one-on-one identification of Eliot's major poetry with Dante seems to fit, that identification was made after the fact, based on Eliot's lifelong admiration for Dante. It ignores Eliot's Puritan ancestry and books like John Bunyan's *Pilgrim's Progress*, in which Christian seeks his own salvation at the expense of family and earthly responsibilities.

There are also early poems in the notebook that can be interpreted in Freudian terms not only as a kind of horror at sexuality, but demonstrating Eliot's confusion over his self-identity. A few critics have seen in him a struggle against unrecognized homosexual leanings because he was afraid of women. Eliot, however, repudiated any such interpretation.

Sometime about 1911 Eliot wrote an agonized poem called "The Love Song of Saint Sebastian," in which he described the war between his spiritual experience of the Absolute and his everyday experience of women, time, and society. The poem suggests that these physical "facts of life" all conspire to keep the young poet from the pure world of the spirit.

Of all these snares, time was always Eliot's worst enemy. It moved so rapidly that he barely saw a bloom before it withered. Women, too, were a source of embarrassment, guilt, and annoyance because, raised in a family where sex was a dirty word, it was closely tied to sin. Despite or perhaps because of a family of energetic, intelligent females, Eliot recorded his annoyance at women's demands, which interfered with his single-minded path toward a "martyrdom," which may have meant a career as a poet.

His approach in these poems, typical of modern poetry, makes it hard to disentangle his poetic and religious goals. In "Easter: Sensations of April," an unpublished poem, some geraniums remind him of a little black girl who brought geraniums from church, where her prayers show she is sure of God. During June 1910 Eliot had a strange experience which he described in another unpublished poem called "Silence." He was walking in Boston when the streets suddenly shrank and divided. In that moment out of time Eliot felt his everyday concerns fall away, leaving him folded in a great silence. Later in an essay on Pascal, Eliot wrote that in daily life such experiences may be communion with the divine. But until science can show us how to reproduce such phenomena, science cannot claim to explain them, and thus we can judge them only by their fruits.

In Eliot's case, no dramatic change occurred in his life at the time, inwardly or outwardly. He again spent the summer at Gloucester writing more poems which expressed his sense of alienation. In a series of satiric poems which he called "Goldfish (Essence of Summer Magazines)" he made fun of his bourgeois existence of flannel suits, tea, and polite conversation. There are similar passages later in his published poems like "Prufrock" and "Portrait of a Lady."

In October 1910 Eliot sailed for France for a year abroad. He was overwhelmed by excitement as he set foot on the Cherbourg docks by moonlight and later called his year in France a "romantic year" in a country that represented "la poesie." He even had the romantic dream of giving up English as a language and becoming a French poet, living abroad and scraping a living as a writer.

Eliot felt that he was lucky to discover Paris as an adolescent—he was actually twenty-two—but his memories are those of a literary adolescent. He went early to get a seat at philosopher Henri Bergson's lectures; he saw Anatole France walking along the dockside; he bought Gide and Claudel's latest books when they first appeared.

Although he never became more than an onlooker of the arts in Paris, Eliot was right about their aura. Paris was the cultural capital of the prewar world, abounding with all the avant-garde art, drama, music, and dance forbidden elsewhere. Famous artists from czarist Russia and the West were there, from Isadora Duncan and the Ballet Russe of Producer Serge Diaghilev to musicians Igor Stravinsky, Richard Strauss, and Claude Debussy. In the theater there was actress Sarah Bernhardt and playwrights Anatole France, Edmond Rostand, Maurice Maeterlinck, and Romain Rolland. The designer Bakst was creating barbaric sets with primary colors for Stravinsky's music, and Paris had just become the home of Italy's self-exiled poet and patriot, Gabriele D'Annunzio.

D'Annunzio's presence may have been especially important to the young Eliot because D'Annunzio was working on a play produced in Paris on May 22, 1911, called *Saint Sebastien*. Although placed on the Roman Catholic Church's Index, *Saint Sebastien* was wildly popular, with critics claiming that d'Annunzio was hiding sensuality under the guise of mysticism. Eliot must have known about the play, which was very like his own unpublished St. Sebastian poem. Some of what in Eliot's notebook appears to be his personal anguish may simply reflect his enthusiastic adoption of Paris's ambiance.

Eliot felt that Paris was far more alive than England or America in

1910, but he decided that the English language had more resources than French. Professor Babbitt had encouraged him to believe that Paris was the intellectual center of the modern world. But Eliot realized that it was not so much the poetic center Yeats dreamed of, as it was the center of rival social ideologies from Durkheim, Remy de Gourmont, Anatole France, Henri Bergson to Charles Maurras, the promoter of order and hierarchy. Paris was also the home of the "disintegrating" work of painters like Matisse and Picasso.

Eliot soon discovered—as many a wishful American student has after him—that as a raw young American he was not privy to the great men or the classic salons he had dreamed about. But he settled in to soak up the things available to a young *inconnu*, playing the observer's role. As he said later, he had "only the genuine stimulus of the place." He knew no one in the literary and artistic world except as spectacles to be seen or listened to on occasion. In fact, he found himself as solitary as he had been in Boston.

Eliot lived in a pension on the Left Bank at 9 Rue de l'Universite. He studied French literature at the Sorbonne and practiced French conversation with Henri Alain-Fournier, young author of *Le Grand Meaulnes*, who was killed early in World War I. Alain-Fournier had introduced Eliot to the work of Dostoyevsky, Gide, and Claudel, but only Dostoyevsky stuck with him. From Dostoyevsky Eliot learned that his own personal defects could be used to enter and describe a "genuine and personal universe." Alain-Fournier introduced Eliot to his brother-in-law and friend, Jacques Riviere, editor of the *Nouvelle Revue Francaise*.

In his pension Eliot met a young medical student named Jean Verdenal. Also interested in literature, Verdenal may have introduced Eliot to the works of Charles Maurras, whose organization and newspaper, both called "Action Francaise," enlisted students called "les Camelots du Roi" to stage demonstrations against plays by Jews and freethinkers. Maurras's movement had grown out of the Dreyfus affair. Maurras himself stood for a nationalistic monarchism, but he ended in prison, accused of being a fascist who by World War II had supported the collaborationist French government of Marshal Petain.

Although, like French writer Jacques Maritain, Eliot greatly admired Maurras's writings, Eliot was no secret activist with a hidden need for violence. Instead, what he appreciated in Maurras's work was his emphasis on the need for order and hierarchy in a cultured and stable society and his admiration for Dante's defense of "Latin" culture.

That year Eliot and Verdenal were friends of the same age who shared intellectual and poetic interests. The suggestion that they had a homosexual relationship is built on slim, ambiguous evidence, primarily the dedication to *Prufrock* and the failure of Eliot's first marriage. Eliot and Verdenal continued to correspond until Verdenal joined the French Army as a medical officer in 1914 and was killed in the Dardanelles in 1915. Eliot dedicated his first volume of poems, *Prufrock and Other Observations*, published in 1917, with an epigraph from Dante, to Verdenal.

Part way through his Parisian year, Eliot's friend from Harvard, Conrad Aiken, appeared. He and Eliot again went for long talks and excursions, learning their way about town. Both read a book which Eliot later wrote conveyed the atmosphere of that prewar Paris, Charles-Louis Philippe's *Bubu de Montparnasse*, a novel about Parisian prostitutes. Reading about it was one thing, but in real life, trying a classic solution for an uptight (or upright) young man—having a casual affair or visiting a prostitute—was not a solution Eliot seems to have tried. Caution for Eliot was always one of the cardinal virtues, even when he feared he might be missing the parade.

Eliot often wandered through the streets of Paris alone, as he had the streets of Boston, looking at the seaminess and squalor, then returning to write poems in his notebook. He began to use a bigger, spiky handwriting, which he dropped once he returned to Boston. His street experiences and emotions appear in the Laforguian poems "Rhapsody on a Windy Night" and parts of "Prufrock" and "Portrait of a Lady." In his unpublished poems Eliot wrote about vigils spent in his room, staring at the stars, trying to ask the "overwhelming question" about the meaning of existence.

Another of Eliot's unpublished poems from the Paris period is about a lost soul in a bar, a kind of ancestor of J. Alfred Prufrock and Gerontion. In several other poems Eliot began to write, indirectly, about God and Christ crucified. Those poems have led some critics to assume that Eliot's "real" conversion to Christianity occurred now. The difficulty with this theory is that only these poetic scraps give any such intimations; no such dramatic change appeared in his life. Instead, Eliot continued to be inwardly confused and unhappy, outwardly poised and proper, playing the role expected of him.

During January and February 1911 Eliot rushed out an hour early to hear the popular Friday lectures by philosopher Henri Bergson at the College de France. Eliot said he had a "temporary conversion to Bergsonism." An effective teacher, Bergson affirmed the relativity of all knowledge and the simultaneity of time, which develops a pattern only through our own introspective memory. The chaos or flux of the world is beyond our knowledge, and we can grasp reality only at rare moments. By 1927, however, Eliot was to criticize Bergson both for his fatalism and relativism.

Eliot went to London briefly in April 1911. He was not impressed by the city or its inhabitants. In "Morning at the Window" he described Londoners living below ground (perhaps in hell) in the typical London basements beneath the streets, hidden by brown waves of fog.

Eliot had hoped to stay in France indefinitely, but that summer, as he and Aiken sat by a Parisian boulevard, sipping *sirop de fraises* (not absinthe) and talking literature, Eliot told his friend he had given up. He was going to return to Harvard in the fall to work toward a doctorate. His decision was probably the result of family pressure, but Eliot, who had written most of his poetry on his own, was going to study philosophy, not literature.

That choice was partly a result of his studies with Babbitt and French philosophers like Bergson, as well as a refusal to teach English literature while trying to write it. It also had an existential purpose in Eliot's mind. Philosophy might teach him to ask the universe the right questions as well as give him a method for organizing his own experience. Eliot was working on a series of poems about a "demented" philosopher to whom nothing seemed real. Later he suggested that such despair could be a kind of mystical experience, a variety of the spiritual journey toward God.

That same summer Eliot visited Munich where he completed and copied into his notebook "The Love Song of J. Alfred Prufrock." Conrad Aiken took a copy with him to London in 1912, but had no success "selling" it to the English avant-garde like Harold Monro, the owner of Poetry Bookshop, who said it was "absolutely insane."

Back in Boston according to Aiken, Eliot had a European manner about him. He took a small room on Ash Street, put in a stove "to point the chairs at," and hung a print of Gauguin's yellow "Crucifixion," which he had bought in Paris. Immaculate as always, he parted his hair behind his ears and carried a cane. He and Aiken continued to meet to talk about poetry and where to write it.

Meanwhile Eliot was studying Sanskrit, Buddhism, and Indian philosophies. An interest in those subjects had been common to the Boston Transcendentalists. More recently, professors Babbitt and Paul Elmer More (who later became a Christian) had studied them, too.

Eliot's later works showed signs of these studies. In *The Waste Land* Eliot drew a red, Indian landscape and used the Thunder God myth for his ending. In "The Dry Salvages" appeared the figures of Krishna and Arjuna. In *The Cocktail Party* the Guardians celebrate a vaguely Eastern ritual. But by spring 1913 Eliot had withdrawn from those courses. He later told a Virginia audience that these studies had left him in a state of "enlightened mystification," and to understand the material he would have to forget to think as an American or a European. For both practical and sentimental reasons, Eliot chose not to do so. His decision showed a solid commitment to Dante's western civilization which Eliot never repudiated.

As a doctoral student Eliot had been appointed to teach under-graduate philosophy courses at Harvard in 1912 and 1913. In 1913 he bought and read Idealist philosopher F. H. Bradley's *Appearance and Reality*, which was to become the basis for his own doctoral thesis. Bradley was one of a group of Oxford Idealist philosophers, recently called the "Magdalen Metaphysicals," who stood out against the prevailing logical positivism of Cambridge's Bertrand Russell and G. E. Moore and who exercised an important influence on C. S. Lewis's thinking.

The spring of 1914 Eliot actually met Bertrand Russell, who was a visiting professor at Harvard; Russell mentioned his pupil Eliot in a letter to his mistress, Lady Ottoline Morrell. Eliot slyly described the satyrlike Russell in his poem "Mr. Apollinax."

While continuing to study and teach, Eliot went on writing poems, completing the four that would make his reputation in 1917: "The Love Song of J. Alfred Prufrock," "Portrait of a Lady," "Rhapsody on a

Windy Night," and "La Figlia che Piange." But he wrote Aiken, to whom he showed most of his work, that he felt his poetry was still "strained and intellectual."

These poems may prove there was something serious about Eliot's relationship with a young Bostonian woman named Emily Hale, whom he met occasionally and corresponded with most of his life. Other proof is lacking because their correspondence is sequestered at Princeton University until A.D. 2020.

A friend of his cousin Eleanor Hinkley, Emily Hale had been raised by an uncle who was a Unitarian minister in Boston. Eliot may have met her as early as 1908. In 1913 he took part in some amateur theatricals with her at his aunt's Cambridge home. Emily was a fine actress who went to college, then taught dramatics, and became an interesting example of a career woman and Bostonian eccentric.

During his last year at Harvard, Eliot also read the lives of the saints and mystics, especially St. Teresa, Dame Julian of Norwich, and St. John of the Cross. He made copious notes on Evelyn Underhill's recent *Mysticism*, noting for his own use her categories of pilgrim, lover, and ascetic. Underhill's monumental "history" of mysticism was based on her romantic perception of the mystical experience as a spiritual adventure that closely resembled falling in love. Her book was heavily influenced by Bergson and his *elan vitale*, which provided an antidote to the depression and despair Eliot fought all his life.

Eliot was preparing to take up a year's traveling fellowship granted him by the philosophy department, no doubt with the expectation that he would return to finish his degree and join the department. But judging from the poems he was writing, with their emphasis on a life of passionate love and self-surrender, Eliot saw himself more like his characters Celia in *The Cocktail Party* and Harry in *The Family Reunion*. Like them he was a passionate pilgrim who needed to break free of family and friends to seek his own spiritual destiny.

His wish to "dare to disturb the universe" by asking the overwhelming question was always in conflict with his diffident terror at the very idea of "being born to play Prince Hamlet" to set the world aright. At any rate, in 1914, neither Eliot nor Evelyn Underhill had any idea of making a public commitment to the institutional Christian church.

PART TWO
Pilgrim 1914 – 1930

CHAPTER FOUR

Expatriate
1914 – 1917

*E*LIOT SAILED AGAIN FOR EUROPE THE SUMMER OF 1914. HE INTENDED
to travel a bit, then go to Oxford to take up his year-long Sheldon
Traveling Fellowship from Harvard. Both his family and the Harvard
faculty expected him to return to finish his thesis and perhaps become
a new star of the Harvard philosophy department.

Whether he would have done so, even if he had returned to America,
is open to question. The Harvard philosophy department had changed
drastically in the past few years. It was moving away from the
metaphysical Idealism of Babbitt and Santayana toward the
Cambridge Realism of G. E. Moore and Bertrand Russell, with its emphasis on mathematics.

Eliot studied the works of those men, but his own philosophical
orientation, like his literary poetics, came from Henri Bergson, F. H.
Bradley, the subject of his dissertation, and Nietzsche's disciples T. E.
Hulme and Remy de Gourmont. Like all these philosophers in their

different ways, Eliot perceived a basic opposition between abstract conventions and immediate experience. Instead of emphasizing one or the other, however, Eliot and his mentor Pound, as Modernist poets, worked to integrate those opposites.

By escaping again to Europe, Eliot probably hoped to gain time and space to resolve his personal dilemma: whether to be a practicing poet or an academic philosopher—with the corollary of how to earn his living. But it is unlikely that Eliot expected to stay abroad permanently; the pull of family expectations and academic obligations was strong. It was outside events and other people that changed the circumstances of his life and turned him into an expatriate.

As if neither he nor his family were aware of current events, Eliot sailed for Europe on June 28, 1914, almost on the day that the Austrian Grand Duke Franz Ferdinand was assassinated in Yugoslavia. World War I was waiting for him in the wings, but, seemingly oblivious, Eliot toured Belgium and Italy, playing the cultivated young American tourist unimpressed by the accepted sights.

By mid-July, Eliot had arrived at Marburg, Germany, where he was scheduled to attend a summer school in philosophy. He wrote to Conrad Aiken that he liked the unkempt rose gardens and excellent meals of his bourgeois landlady, and, relaxing a bit, left the issue of his future to itself.

He began to plan a long poem to be called "The Descent from the Cross," constructed (like most of his major works) out of fragments and shorter poems. In it Eliot used the ironic tone and violent juxtapositions of Laforgue. In the '20s Ezra Pound wanted to publish one section called "The Death of Saint Narcissus," but Eliot killed it at the galley stage. Like Virginia Woolf in her writing, Eliot exercised great self-control about his work, reworking poems over long periods of time and never publishing them if he felt they were unsatisfactory. "Saint Narcissus," a consciously "religious" poem about a self-immolating martyr, did appear much later in *Poems of Early Youth*.

When war broke out in August, the world took charge of Eliot's plans. Only two weeks after he arrived in Germany, he had to leave very hurriedly for London via Rotterdam. Under similar circumstances Dorothy L. Sayers found herself nearly stranded in France. She returned to Oxford to find university life taking on the confusions, emptiness, and alarms of war. Ironically, however, as she later testified, since women students were not really a part of university life, there was little likelihood that Eliot, who complained that he missed the company of bright women, might meet her there. Sayers herself did not become acquainted with other young poets until she worked at Blackwell's after the war.

Both Sayers and Eliot have been accused of not taking World War I seriously. Neither dashed off to enlist or openly suffered great personal losses; in 1914 both stuck to their appointed tasks. But Sayers later married a war veteran whose health was permanently affected. By 1917 Eliot had lost not only his French friend, Jean Verdenal, but also the closest friend he was to make at Oxford, a young historian named Carl Culpin. When America entered the war, Eliot did try to enlist. Both he and Sayers were clearly aware of the loss of so many of their generation and suffered the postwar moods of silliness and despair. World War I may not have left them with the emotional scars of a Lewis or Tolkien, who fought, but it left them with the sense of guilt and depression common to survivors.

When Eliot arrived at London in August 1914, the city still did not appeal to him. But London marked the turning point in Eliot's life because that fall he met Ezra Pound. As has been noted, Conrad Aiken, who had a more highly developed sense of public relations (and may have thought that touting his clever friend would help him as well) had already shown Eliot's poem, "The Love Song of J. Alfred Prufrock," to some of London's literary world without success.

Then Aiken met another expatriate American poet, the thirty-year-old, flamboyant, red-bearded Ezra Pound. Pound had been in London for five years and had published five volumes of poetry. Brash, eccentric, and energetic, he had managed to make himself the center of the circles developing new literary and cultural ideas. Pound told Aiken to send Eliot to see him when he came to London.

Possibly from nervousness, since Pound was already well known, Eliot put off visiting him until September 22, 1914. Then he came to take tea in Pound's tiny, triangular drawing room in Kensington. According to poet and painter Wyndham Lewis, whom Eliot met there, this was the only room with a window in Pound's dark apartment.

Eliot was quiet and low-voiced but perfectly self-possessed.

Wyndham Lewis, who painted two famous portraits of Eliot, described him in 1914 as tall, sleek, and attractive, with a "Gioconda smile" and the remnants of an American drawl. Pound told his guest to send him some poems, so Eliot sent him "Portrait" and "Prufrock."

Pound was impressed by these poems and began a campaign to get Harriet Monroe, editor of *Poetry*, to publish them. Pound wrote Monroe that Eliot was a marvel because he had "trained and modernized himself on his own." A combination of the enthusiastic American and a natural impresario, Pound proceeded to give Eliot an entree to the London world of letters. He introduced Eliot to Wyndham Lewis with his Vortex magazine *Blast* and Harriet Weaver of *The Egoist*, where Eliot was to publish articles.

Pound now undertook Eliot's "education," telling his new protégé to read T. E. Hulme and Remy de Gourmont. Pound and Eliot also agreed that Dante was the greatest poet of Western civilization (Chesterton's *Christendom*). Pound had quickly picked up the Dantean echoes in Eliot's "Prufrock," and he encouraged Eliot to continue to study Dante's complete work.

Physically, Pound was almost the opposite of the immaculate, conservatively dressed, and languid young Eliot. Pound never sat still. He uttered strange cries and waved his pince-nez when excited. He wore a swashbuckling cape and carried a stick in the Chestertonian manner. Pound liked to show off his protégés in public, and Eliot quietly and graciously cooperated.

Fortunately for Eliot, Pound regarded it as his mission to improve and modernize English literature. He had grown up in Idaho in a family which, like Eliot's, originated in Puritan New England. He had gone to an eastern college and had taught in American universities before escaping abroad.

Unlike Pound, however, Eliot did not judge America solely by how it treated its writers, although he was not impressed by its ruling literary clique. Like Pound, he also felt that American literature either derived from Europe or ignored it. Eliot and Pound were very conscious of an artist's relationship to his own nationality and to civilization. Both were seeking a sense of tradition and order, but they also yearned for a return to the more homogenous America of their ancestors. As old men, however, Pound and Eliot, who had been the trailblazing forerunners of the postwar exodus of writers like Stein, Hemingway, and Fitzgerald, were to declare that they now felt themselves to be American writers.

Pound and Eliot had developed similar agendas for poetry. By developing Modernism, which was both a poetics and a philosophy that emphasized the sharp difference between the conscious surfaces and unconscious depths of experience, Pound and Eliot revolutionized English verse—although it was Eliot who made Modernism respectable. Modernism in philosophy was characterized by the tension between abstract and immediate experience, and in poetry by swift perceptions and abrupt juxtapositions of unrelated particulars. The poets then used metaphor and irony to create new and unexpected relationships.

Eliot and Pound did not meet often; in October 1914 Eliot left London for Merton College, Oxford. But they began a lifelong exchange of letters, in which Pound made sweeping statements, and Eliot responded cautiously and precisely. At Oxford, Eliot was expected to study Aristotle under the tutorship of Professor Harold Joachim. Joachim was an Idealist philosopher and a disciple of F. H. Bradley. Although still at Merton, Bradley lived like a recluse, so Eliot never met him.

By contrast to C. S. Lewis and Dorothy L. Sayers, for example, who found Oxford an earthly paradise, Eliot liked it even less than London. Like Charles Williams, he was an urbanite who appreciated gothic architecture, but, as he wrote Conrad Aiken, he did not want to be "dead" (entombed in libraries or exiled from the theater and arts of the capital). Not raised in a single-sex society, Eliot also did not want to live in an exclusively masculine environment where general social conversation was lacking. He also found the ancient colleges damp and chilly. A young poet later recalled that Eliot, with his dry humor, had solemnly recommended he take long woolen underwear to Oxford.

In spite of the wartime call-up of most able-bodied young men, the life of a male student at Oxford was still gentlemanly and leisured. Eliot studied hard, but he also played tennis, went to parties, joined some clubs, and even rowed for his College. He won a pewter mug inscribed with the name of the crew, which he proudly displayed for many years. He also read "Prufrock" publicly for the first time to a small group called the Coterie.

Eliot later said that his tutor, Joachim, had taught him to write good English prose. Eliot now began to compose on a typewriter, often working standing up. He said it made his writing more lucid, if not more subtle. As he studied Aristotle, Eliot also worked on his dissertation on Bradley, which he completed in 1916 but did not publish until 1964.

There has been considerable disagreement about Bradley's influence on Eliot's work. Some take Eliot's comment in 1964, that he found his thesis painfully obscure, as proof that Idealist philosophy only expressed his skepticism about the relationship between mind and reality, and showed his need to resolve his personal sense of disintegration. Others feel that Bradley was responsible for some of Eliot's basic artistic and philosophical ideas and helped Eliot become the acknowledged master of a new synthesis that successfully combined philosophy and poetry.

Eliot's studies at Oxford probably were vital to his role of philosopher poet for two reasons. First, through his studies with Joachim, he was brought into intellectual fellowship with a group of men who formed a chain of inheritance that preserved into the '30s and '40s the Idealist concern to reunite philosophy and theology. That concern was at the root of the Christian apologetic of both C. S. Lewis and Eliot. Second, Eliot's interpretation of Bradley's Idealism is embedded in Modernist poetics, where it affected both Eliot's poetry and criticism.

Four twentieth-century scholars at Magdalen College, Oxford— Clement Webb, John Alexander Smith, R. G. Collingwood, and C. S. Lewis—came to be called the "Magdalen Metaphysicals," because their philosophical Idealism emphasized poetry and myth. They too admired Eliot's favorite seventeenth-century poets: Donne, Cowley, Crashaw, and Herbert. At the time, Oxford had become convinced that language itself was too vague for philosophical use, but scholars still shared an interest in classics and history and a belief that philosophy was essentially literary, with close ties to poetry. For them religion might begin with experience, but it was ultimately a matter of intellectual truth, and they were confident there was a relationship between intellectual and moral life. They all sought to reunite joy, reason, and virtue, a quest they thought came from a natural longing for an Absolute whose object is not in this world.

Three of the four were orthodox Christians, who devoted part of their professional careers to apologetics. Ironically, although "classicist" Eliot was one of their disciples, they called their philosophy "romantic." As early as 1917, when Eliot had established himself in London, he wrote reviews praising books by Webb and Collingwood. They all expressed their conviction that Christianity was true, not merely satisfying, and, despite C. S. Lewis's distrust of Eliot's neo-scholasticism, once they had accepted Christianity, were facing a common enemy.

A study of the root of Modernism points to a related significance of Bradleyan philosophy in Eliot's work. Modernism made use of the interrelationship between literary, psychological, and philosophical ideas current at the beginning of the twentieth century. The opposition between abstraction and experience found in Idealist philosophy resembled the surfaces and depths of Modernist poetry. It was probably Nietzsche, meditated through Hulme and de Gourmont, who gave Eliot the idea of using metaphor as the connection between abstract and immediate experience, as well as the way to create new forms. Both Bradley and Nietzsche had emphasized the Modernist credo of the impersonality of the artist, the swiftness of perceptions, and the independence of the text itself from the biography of the writer. Pound and Eliot in turn, in their use of these concepts, were to influence I. A. Richards and Cleanth Brooks and the development of the "New Criticism" of the '30s and '40s.

Bradley's philosophy also helps explain the source of some of Eliot's key terms in his early criticism—for example, the term *objective correlative*. By "objective correlative," Eliot meant that a poet should transform an emotion into an object or event that evoked the emotion. Eliot insisted that he held an impersonal, objective (or "classical") view of art, but recent critics have insisted that he was actually engaged in personal expression. It appears that what Eliot really wanted to create was a poetry that could unite the two. Closely influenced by early twentieth-century art, music, and drama, Eliot, like Pound, saw the modern arts as disrupting ordinary ways of looking and speaking, not to divorce art from life, but to develop a new method to organize experience.

While he worked at developing these ideas, during his second term at Oxford in February 1915, Eliot heard from Harvard that they had granted him a fellowship for a second year. The grant made him realize that he did not want to go on being a student. He did not like either wartime London or Oxford, and his family, who had been supporting him for ten years, insisted that he return and go to work. Eliot had been having trouble writing new poems, and he toyed with the idea of going to live in wartime Paris as a way of working through his writer's block.

One deciding factor in his decision to stay but not continue his academic work was Ezra Pound. Pound was working overtime on Eliot's behalf, and Eliot knew there was a real possibility that his poetry would be published in England, where it would find a more receptive audience than at home. Then, during the course of 1915, Pound managed to get all of Eliot's completed poems into print, and Eliot began to compose again.

While finishing the year at Oxford, Eliot wrote his "Boston" poems "Cousin Nancy" and "The Boston Evening Transcript," which appeared in *Poetry* that August. Wyndham Lewis published Eliot's "Preludes" and "Rhapsody on a Windy Night" in his little magazine *Blast*. Eliot's "Portrait of a Lady" appeared in America in *Others*, and five Eliot poems came out in Pound's *Catholic Anthology* that November.

The most important of Eliot's early poems, "The Love Song of J. Alfred Prufrock," was published in Chicago in the back pages of *Poetry* that June. Eliot, who, like many writers enjoyed later laying down the law about his own work and redefining his intentions, said that Prufrock represented a split personality, half a middle-aged man, half himself. As the timid, balding lover, Prufrock is a Jamesian character, full of the airs and graces of a proper Bostonian at a tea party. As Eliot the poet, Prufrock is the equally timid seeker of the Absolute, scared to disturb the universe by asking it the "overwhelming question." Although written in Laforguian style, its Dantean echoes led to the poem's being called Eliot's *Hell* and a milestone on Eliot's route to the Christianity he mocked and doubted.

But it was not only his sudden, modest success in literature and Pound's exuberant patronage that changed the direction of Eliot's life. It was his sudden marriage. Summer term at Oxford Eliot had met Vivien (or Vivienne) Haigh-Wood, a friend of Scofield Thayer's sister. A former Harvard classmate now at Oxford, Thayer later published Eliot's poems in *The Dial*. Eliot and Vivien probably met in Thayer's college rooms or at a party on the river.

Vivien, who aspired to be a ballet dancer, was the child of an upper-middle-class painter. She was small, dark, bright, and talkative. The London literary world intrigued her, but she was also a "flapper" and something of a flirt, fond of bohemian clothes, dancing, and parties. Bertrand Russell gossiped that she was "vulgar" and that Eliot had married beneath him, neither of which was really true.

Eliot clearly fell in love with her. Vivien was on the rebound from another love affair. She found Eliot good-looking in an unusual sort of way and their mutual friends were already talking about Eliot's potential as a poet. On the surface, they seemed to be just what the other needed. As Russell, whom Eliot had just met again in London, suggested, Eliot thought Vivien would help him to break out of his solemn shell, and Vivien confidently expected to liven him up and be his poetic inspiration.

Just what precipitated their hasty marriage is not known, but it was probably inevitable. Eliot's Puritan upbringing made it very unlikely that, having reached age twenty-seven without having an affair, he would do so now. If he loved her, he would want to marry her. At the same time, Pound was urging the marriage, hoping it would keep Eliot in London under his wing.

But they had known one another only two months, and neither of them had any financial resources beyond their families, when they went to the London registry office on June 26, 1915, to be married. Neither one told their parents until they returned from their brief honeymoon to face Vivien's parents in Hampstead. Her parents were fairly easily reconciled. Eliot's never really were because they suspected that marriage to an Englishwoman would keep Eliot abroad.

Unknown to Eliot until after their marriage, Vivien had an ominous history of depression and wild moods, which were being controlled by drugs. Some sort of hormonal imbalance contributed to her chronic bad health. Although Eliot assumed responsibility for her financial and medical support and put much effort into taking care of her, he seems to have given up too quickly trying to bridge the gap between them, whereas Vivien never really believed it existed. They did not complement one another's temperaments.

Bored when Eliot worked long hours, Vivien wanted attention. Eliot needed the privacy of his own soul. If she was moody and demanding,

Eliot was obliged to work hard to support them and make a success of his writing, and he had suffered all his life from lack of energy. But there is no doubt that in a sense he regarded himself as having "murdered" her. With their temperamental and physical incompatibilities, it seems incredible that they managed to live together as long as they did, especially since Eliot suffered great guilt about her as well as for having betrayed his parents' hopes for him.

Some critics have suggested that Vivien's literary talent was sacrificed on the altar of his, but it is difficult to see how Eliot could have played the custodial role of a Leonard Woolf and written much himself. Many of Eliot's intellectual acquaintances snubbed Vivien, but Vivien clearly did have literary ability which Eliot made some effort to encourage. He also accepted her advice about his own poetry.

At first their life worked, after a fashion. In many ways Eliot felt more alive and involved with the real world than he had ever been, and he set about reorganizing his life to earn their living. He sailed back to America in July 1915 to make his peace with his startled, unhappy parents. Vivien refused to go, afraid of both German submarines and America, and she refused to consider living there. Eliot's father was disapproving, but he continued Eliot's small allowance. Eliot's mother, who had expected him to fulfill her ambitions in her way, was more upset. Ironically, she even wrote to Bertrand Russell to ask him to encourage Eliot to continue in philosophy, rather than try to earn a living writing *vers libre*. To please his parents, Eliot agreed to finish his doctoral thesis, even though it took what free time he had for writing.

On Eliot's return to London the young couple quit living with Vivien's parents in Hampstead and moved to a small apartment where they were guests of Bertrand Russell. Hard up as they were, this odd arrangement did not work well. Russell, who was between wives, although well supplied with mistresses, flirted with Vivien and entertained her while Eliot worked; it is possible he actually seduced her. At the same time, playing the benefactor, Russell introduced Eliot to other literary circles such as the Bloomsbury Group and gave Eliot some bonds in a company making arms which paid them a small dividend. As soon as he could, Eliot paid him back.

Although Pound was getting Eliot's poems published to acclaim within the London literary worlds, they could not live on love, especially with Vivien's medical bills. To support them, Eliot turned to school teaching. His first job was as a master at High Wycombe Grammar School, which required a long commute from London, for 140 pounds a year, plus lunch.

Like many would-be writers, Aldous Huxley and Dorothy Sayers among them, Eliot hoped beforehand that it would be easy to teach things he already knew, and that he would have plenty of free time for writing. What he discovered was that in order to teach he had to project his personality on the students, with the result that he was too exhausted to write, even during school holidays. He was never a "natural ham," despite his quiet sense of fun. What Eliot enjoyed most was playing at being "the Aged Eagle" or "Old Possum."

On the other hand, holding a regular job with steady pay was more natural (and less unnerving) for Eliot the Puritan than to try to survive by writing poetry, doing freelance reviewing and editing, or accepting handouts from others. To the consternation of his London literary friends, he continued to be a regular wage earner all his life. It helped him establish his own discipline as well as maintain self-respect. He also found he could not write more than three hours a day and do work he found acceptable.

After one term Eliot changed schools to teach at Highgate Junior School. This school was closer to their home and paid twenty pounds a year more. Here Eliot taught the future poet laureate, Sir John Betjeman, who recalled him as the quiet American master.

But Eliot needed more money than he made from schoolteaching and parental subsidy. He began to work evenings as an extension lecturer, teaching adult courses in literature. Much of the material he taught found its way into his critical essays written during the next few years. Eliot was a competent lecturer and found it satisfying work, but he did not have Charles Williams' charismatic ability to make disciples of his students.

Again through the good offices (or guilty conscience) of Bertrand Russell, Eliot began to write book reviews. His first ones appeared in philosophical journals where he reviewed books by the "Magdalen Metaphysicals," then in the *Manchester Guardian* and the *New Statesman*, and finally in the *Times Literary Supplement*. It was in these early essays that Eliot developed his critical voice: intellectual, acute, and ironic, which he described as "the braggadocio of the mild-mannered man safely entrenched behind his typewriter."

Busy as he was, Eliot completed his doctoral thesis. He planned to defend it at Harvard in April 1916 but Vivien refused to go to America and fought to keep him from going (this was just before the sinking of the *Lusitania*, which helped to bring America into the war). Then the boat on which Eliot had passage was cancelled. As a result, he simply sent his thesis to Harvard, where it was accepted, but he was never granted his degree.

The Eliots now found a place of their own near Baker Street. Eliot knew and liked the stories of Sherlock Holmes, but this place was not very comfortable, nor was wartime London, with its air raids, black-outs, and shortages of food and fuel. On the other hand, Eliot was becoming a real part of the London literary world.

By 1916 Eliot had met Clive Bell, one of the young men of the Bloomsbury Group who were serving as farm hands because of their conscientious objector status. They worked at Garsington, the country home of Lady Ottoline Morrell. Although Eliot became good friends with Virginia and Leonard Woolf, most of the Bloomsbury lions treated him as a kind of family joke, bored by what they saw as his self-pitying worries, formal manners, and precise way of speaking. Cosmopolitan in interests, the Bloomsbury Group were still incurably English, and by birth and education were still securely part of the establishment. Eliot the American would always be an outsider, even if he dressed and spoke like a proper native.

Bloomsbury, however, did recognize Eliot's literary gifts as soon as they heard Katherine Mansfield read "Prufrock" aloud at an Easter party at Garsington in 1917. For his part, Eliot accepted their support and shared part of their literary agenda, but he refused to be patronized by them. His friends like Pound and Wyndham Lewis heartily disapproved of "Blooomsbury" as both highbrow and affected.

At the end of 1916 Eliot quit schoolteaching to try to live on lecturing and reviews. Pound recommended him to the editor of the American *Little Review*. Eliot, however, did not become a regular contributor, although he published a difficult but amusing couple of dialogues between Eeldrop (Eliot) and Appleplex (Pound) and a few other poems there. Still, Eliot did not find enough freelance work to support himself and his wife. Worried about money, he found himself again unable to write. Then in March 1917, through a friend of Vivien's parents, he got a job working at Lloyds Bank in the City.

CHAPTER FIVE

The Waste Land
1917 – 1922

*E*LIOT STAYED AT LLOYDS BANK FOR EIGHT YEARS, STEADILY RISING
in its colonial and foreign department. Having a steady job freed him
from much of his financial anxiety, and he began to write poetry
again, although at first only in French. It had taken only three months
as a freelancer to teach him that he was better off emotionally with a
secure source of income. The previous year had also shown him, as
Dorothy Sayers learned about the same time, that schoolteaching was
far too strenuous and demanding for a writer. (Neither tried the life of
a university professor, which might have given them more time, but
would have kept them in a more cloistered atmosphere which neither
sought.)

What appeared to be Yankee caution paid off handsomely in a
remarkably short time. Staying and working in London, Eliot was in
the right place at the right time and did the right things to be noticed.
Although he later admitted it had been a period of incredible strain,

within five years he had taken over the leadership of the coming literary generation.

In letters to family and friends, Eliot complained a great deal about having too much to do and too little energy or time to do it. In spite of his deliberate manner, which was partly the result of a physical clumsiness (noticed by his friend William Levy), Eliot was always a worrier, sure he would miss a train or forget his ticket. His fussing about overwork, however, was justified; with his job, extension lecturing, editing, and writing, Eliot worked ten- to fourteen-hour days. But the complaints in diaries or letters are also a release for a writer, who can return refreshed to his "real work," so the evidence they provide is only part of the story. Many of his letters reveal Eliot enjoying himself by communicating with someone else interested in his writing.

His London literary friends, including Ezra Pound, took his tales of woe too seriously. They never understood that the bank job meant not only financial security, but that an Eliot was not raised to be a dilettante. An Eliot was expected to earn his living, and then in his spare time participate in the arts or do good works for the benefit of the community.

Eliot's short period of freelancing not only upset his writing, but it did not help the problems of his marriage. He felt responsible for supporting the two of them, but he was unwilling to give up the hope of being a successful poet. Vivien Eliot wanted her husband to be a recognized poet, too, but she was less able to face the fact that this future depended on Eliot's working and writing at the same time. Her medical bills made her nervous about their financial situation, and she also resented the fact that his parents were not prepared to support her and Tom indefinitely.

Both sets of parents were contributing something at this point, but here their different backgrounds came into play. It was more of an English than American custom for middle-class parents to provide grown children with allowances. Eliot also never believed that the world had an obligation to support him because he was an artist.

Meanwhile, as Eliot struggled with his overextended workload, Vivien had little to do and was often unhappy. This upset Eliot, who in turn would fall ill, and she would become upset by that—creating a vicious circle that occurred over and over during their married life. When she felt well, she was unable to get a government job because she was married to an alien. Eliot did not want her to try for an ordinary job because the daily routine would be very difficult when she had headaches and sleepless nights.

According to Eliot's scoffing literary friends, he now looked the part of a "confidential clerk," wearing a dark suit and carrying a rolled umbrella. His conservative attire led Virginia Woolf to write Clive Bell that Eliot would be there, wearing a "four-piece suit." In her letters and diary Woolf sharpened her claws on Eliot, as she did on almost everyone else, but she also became a friend whose literary judgment he respected. The Eliots' busy social life was dominated by these literary connections, which were crucial for his literary success, but Vivien found literary gatherings very difficult.

Friends who visited Eliot at Lloyds Bank found him at work in a murky, greenish basement office beneath the sidewalk, with footsteps echoing overhead. Eliot sat hunched (he habitually sat round-shouldered with bent head, cigarette in hand) over a big table covered with correspondence. One Eliot admirer, a young English professor from Cambridge, met a senior Lloyds officer who asked him if Eliot's poetry was any good. When assured that it was, the banker was delighted because he felt that if a man was really keen on his hobby— no matter what it was—it made him a better worker. He added that Eliot might end up a branch manager and when this was reported back to Eliot, he was quite pleased.

Working in the City, Eliot typically ate lunch at a local chop house, then might spend part of his lunch hour visiting some of the many handsome Wren churches, or crossing the Thames on London Bridge to look back at the dingy wharves contrasting with the graceful spires. Other days Eliot began what became a lifelong habit of luncheon meetings with friends and collaborators to discuss literary projects.

By April 1917 the United States entered the war. Although he had not been accepted for active service before, Eliot wrote his father that he was escaping the trial of his generation and again tried to enlist. Red tape snarled his efforts, and it was fall 1918 before he finally was offered a job in U. S. Naval Intelligence. He quit the bank, sat about for several weeks waiting his orders, and then, needing the money, got reinstated at the bank just as the Armistice was declared.

During the transitional time in London as the war wound grimly down, Eliot had completed making the literary connections that would make him the dominant voice in poetry and criticism by the mid '20s. He became a contributor to or editor for a number of "little magazines." Compared to Pound, with his exotic appearance and pro-American slant (work Pound liked went first to *Poetry* in Chicago and later to *The Dial*, also American), Eliot now appeared safely English. American poet William Carlos Williams might grumble that Eliot's "incongruously correct attire" was a "gesture of contempt" for the Americans of the Lost Generation living *la vie boheme*, but it was really Eliot's natural taste, combined with clever protective coloration.

In June 1917 Eliot added to his other duties the job of literary editor of Harriet Weaver's little magazine the *Egoist*, begun as a feminist sheet. Pound had been its literary editor, and he got this job for Eliot; in fact, part of Eliot's salary was secretly financed by Pound. Eliot kept the job until 1919, when the *Egoist* folded. The *Egoist* published Modernist essays and literature. It serialized James Joyce's *Portrait of the Artist* and Wyndham Lewis's *Tarr*. Eliot's most famous critical essay, "Tradition and the Individual Talent" would be published there.

It was in the *Egoist* that Eliot first publicly attacked the Georgian "Old Guard" of Arnold Bennett, George Bernard Shaw, H. G. Wells, and John Galsworthy, specifically with reference to G. K. Chesterton, a world-famous writer and Christian apologist. Chesterton was actually struggling to keep alive his brother Cecil's little weekly newspaper, but Eliot announced that he saw Chesterton riding on a white horse at the head of the forces of death (showing he had read Chesterton's epic *The Ballad of the White Horse*). Those forces (death-dealing, Eliot believed, to the English language) were the writers whom he called decadent descendants of nineteenth-century Liberal Romanticism. By contrast Eliot said that Joyce, Pound, and Wyndham Lewis, whom Lewis called "The Men of 1914," were writing "living English."

As a critic, Eliot now discarded his collegiate pose as the leisured young gentleman of letters to lead the attack on the prevailing amateur attitude toward poetry and literary criticism. What Eliot now proclaimed was the high seriousness of the role of the professional poet-critic. He saw himself as a craftsman who was talking about a trade that he practiced himself.

Eliot's position taking art to be a high calling was widely shared by many of his generation. Writers as different as Dorothy L. Sayers and Virginia Woolf took the role of writer, and of doing the right work, very seriously. Although Woolf saw herself as freed from her past in a way Sayers never did, she was a direct descendant of the Clapham Sect, a high-minded, social reform, evangelical group of writers, ministers, and politicians, who were not so different from Eliot's family. They had inculcated in Woolf her strong moral sense, which she used to defend the high calling of art for art's sake in a fragmented world.

Meanwhile, by June 1917 Ezra Pound had chosen twelve of Eliot's recent poems and persuaded Harriet Weaver to publish them in a small book called *Prufrock and Other Observations*. Unknown to Eliot, the cost of the printing was paid by Weaver and Pound's wife Dorothy. It took three years to sell out the five hundred copies at a shilling each. *Prufrock*'s reviews were not spectacular, but it found a small, influential audience who saw themselves in its lonely, alienated beings, struggling in a mad world with the existential question of meaning.

Prufrock now was "discovered" by a number of literary hopefuls and returning servicemen, among them I. A. Richards of Cambridge University, Herbert Read, and Bonamy Dobrée. Still younger readers found that Eliot's poetry helped them know their world imaginatively. Eliot won their allegiance for *Prufrock*, who may be damned for not daring to disturb the universe but was also self-deprecating and comical.

Among the majority who disliked Eliot's verse was serviceman C. S. Lewis. Returning to Oxford, Lewis was disgruntled to find most of his Oxford contemporaries quite taken with the new verse, which he called "clever" and "seasick." In spite of Lewis's fulminations, an important source of Eliot's growing role as literary arbiter was to be the study and admiration of his work by the academic world, especially in England, but later in America as well.

Oxford and Cambridge had only recently allowed students to "read" English for a degree. Unlike the young dons J. R. R. Tolkien and C. S. Lewis, who wanted to concentrate on past centuries, others like I. A. Richards were eager for "modern material" to which their war-weary students would more readily respond. Within ten years a Cambridge undergraduate wrote that, just as on entering an Anglican church, visitors were given *The Book of Common Prayer* and *Hymns Ancient and Modern*, on entering

Cambridge, students were given Eliot's poems and criticism.

A few years later Richards tried to persuade Eliot to consider a professorship at Cambridge but Eliot turned it down. Like Chesterton before him, Eliot preferred the freedom of being a man of letters. But Richards's support for Eliot's work helped him and allowed the fledgling English departments to claim that modern English literature was an intellectual, even ethical discipline. The same process was later repeated in America under the aegis of Allen Tate and Cleanth Brooks.

In June 1918 Pound's American benefactor, New Yorker John Quinn, arranged for Knopf to publish Eliot's essay "Ezra Pound, His Metric and Poetry." Written to coincide with the publication of Pound's poems, Eliot's essay was unsigned, so it would not seem to be "too obvious a ping-pong match."

That essay illustrated Eliot's use of criticism to "lay down the law," as well as his technique for subtly undercutting the arrogance of his pronouncements with wit and a deft use of quotation. In this essay, using Chestertonian methods, Eliot turned the attack on Pound on its head by pushing his argument to extremes to make his point. He first showed that Pound was a capable craftsman, not a pedantic scholar who used obscure quotations. Eliot next begged the issue of free verse by insisting that Pound was saving the modern world from Romanticism by creating (Classical) order in his poetry. Then Eliot praised *Poetry* for publishing that most "traditional" of poetic forms, the epic.

In late 1918 Eliot was given the job of sorting out war debts owed the bank, a task that made him drearily aware of the problems of peace and the Treaty of Versailles. Vindictive and unenforceable, the treaty worked against Eliot's dream of a reunified European civilization. Its postwar settlement was denounced by critics as diverse as the young Bloomsbury economist John Maynard Keynes and old liberal Chesterton, all of whom saw personal greed as the keynote dominating the peace conference and its aftermath. No job as editor on a little literary magazine could have made so real to Eliot the "waste land" of Western civilization, caught between the destruction of the war and the devastation of the peace.

Also in November 1918, as the postwar world came into being, Eliot paid his first visit to the Woolfs in their Sussex home called Monk's House. The Woolfs were considering publishing Eliot's poems, but

Virginia continued to tease him in writing and to his face, calling him "Poor Tom" or "Great Tom." It took Woolf a long time to discover that Eliot had a sense of humor. Ironically, many people were frightened of Woolf, but Eliot showed no such signs. Part of the reason may be that she had already admired his serious poetry when she and her friends were hardly known except as artists. Her only published novel was *The Voyage Out*, Keynes had not yet dissected the economic follies of the time, and Lytton Strachey had not yet demythologized the art of biography with his *Eminent Victorians*. Early in their friendship Eliot told the Woolfs that he really wanted to compose a poetic drama which would star characters like those in his Sweeney poems.

In December 1918 Eliot came one noon from the bank to a benefit poetry reading, which was satirically described by Aldous Huxley. Huxley also took part, together with Osbert Sitwell, and other "younger" lesser-known poets. When Eliot was scolded by Sir Edmund Gosse for being late he showed no annoyance but politely read some of his latest poems. One was "The Hippopotamus." This sardonic, "antireligious" poem was much appreciated by novelist Arnold Bennett, who invited Eliot to come see him.

By 1919 Eliot was working for John Middleton Murry's *Athenaeum* and doing unsigned reviews for the *Times Literary Supplement*. In these papers Eliot was reaching a larger audience and learning about the work of editors. But he refused to quit the bank to take on the editorship of the *Athenaeum*, fearing the magazine's lack of financial security. He also felt that being obliged to write, just to fill up a paper, would destroy him as a writer.

With the help of Pound and his patron, Eliot had been trying to get the Prufrock poems published in a book in the United States. Eliot desperately wanted to show his doubting father he was not wasting his talents in England, but early in 1919 his father died. Eliot had been planning to visit his family; now he had not only lost the chance to see his father again but also had an added sense of guilt and failure.

Meanwhile, as he was working hard and growing in literary stature Eliot was revising bits of poetry, some written as early as 1914. These fragments lacked the ironic note of his more recent poems. Some dealt with modern marriage, some with spiritual experiences, some with living in a foreign city—variations on the theme of being cast into a contemporary limbo or hell. The writings of the saints, the "chosen" in the Puritan sense, still intrigued Eliot; the fragments show his readings in Dante, St. Augustine, and St. John of the Cross. Together with "Gerontion," these bits formed the nucleus of a long poem Eliot had promised as a New Year's resolution to his mother and John Quinn.

Eliot wrote "Gerontion" during May and June 1919. This poem was created from the same material as *The Waste Land*, where Eliot had originally included the poem. In addition to late Elizabethan and Jacobean playwrights like Webster and Tourneur, Eliot had begun to read the seventeenth-century Anglican sermons of Donne, Latimer, and Andrewes, all masters of the English language. In "Gerontion" Eliot used their vocabulary, talking of vice, virtues, devils, and faith—and a biblical waiting in the desert for a sign. Eliot even used a phrase of Andrewes's that "We would see a sign."

In his poem, Gerontion, a little old man, is a wry, dried-up evangelist whose modern knowledge has not saved him. Gerontion's vision is an understated description of his inner emptiness. His lack of belief means that he must face God's judgment in "Christ the tiger." Gerontion lives in a dingy boarding house, which, like Shaw's prewar *Heartbreak House*, is the desolate city, Europe itself. The poem moves from personal history to the contemporary world, then to time itself, which was to be a continuing spiritual preoccupation of Eliot's generation.

Poems 1919 was published in May by the Woolfs' Hogarth Press, but Eliot was exhausted by his job, evening lecturing, and poetry writing. Because the Eliots' small noisy apartment got on both their nerves, Vivien spent the summer of 1919 in a country cottage trying to improve her health, while Eliot spent three weeks in France, walking and sightseeing with Ezra Pound. Eliot even grew a beard. Back in London by October 1919 Eliot began to fit together the pieces of poetry he had been working on. He tentatively called his projected poem, "He Do the Police in Different Voices."

By February 1920 Eliot's second poetry collection, called *Ara Voc Prec*, had been published in England; the title was a quotation from Dante. At the same time, in America Knopf finally brought out all of Eliot's "finished" poems. These included "Gerontion," "Sweeney Among the Nightingales," "The Hippopotamus," and "Whispers of Immortality." People who prefer Eliot's sarcastic, detached verse often regard them as better than his so-called religious poems. The quatrains of the latter three, and others, modeled on Pound's work, have a kind of art deco quality reminiscent of Edith Sitwell.

In several poems Eliot was attacking the institutional church's smugness and hypocrisy, using his memories of Unitarian churches. But, however scathing he sounded, clearly he was still concerned with religious practices. "Mr. Eliot's Sunday Morning Service" was the most obvious, but Pound's favorite, "The Hippopotamus" is a mock-Epistle in which Eliot compares the translated river god to the True Church. In "Whispers of Immortality" he talks of the playwright Webster, who "saw the skull beneath the skin," and about the poet Donne, obsessed by death and mortality.

After trying again to raise money to rescue Eliot from the bank, Pound himself left England for good. He had become dissatisfied with London, where his manners and lack of compromise made him unpopular, and defiantly took off for Paris. As a result, the place he might have occupied in postwar London literature was taken by his protégé Eliot.

Eliot warned Pound that, compared to London, Paris was not a city where he would associate with many first-class writers who were making names for themselves or remaking English literature. But, as Eliot wrote John Quinn, Pound kept antagonizing people who could help him. Pound and others retorted that Eliot was much too careful not to put a foot wrong, even in a good cause. Pound, however, continued to be involved in Eliot's career.

By August 1920, Eliot, who had suffered his first bad attack of bronchitis the previous December, took off again for France. This time he traveled with Wyndham Lewis whom Vivien Eliot persuaded to go along to make sure Eliot took care of himself. In Paris, Eliot and Lewis met James Joyce, another Pound protégé. Eliot told Lewis he thought Joyce was arrogant because he was convinced that the world ought to be at work on his behalf. Wyndham Lewis thought that this was pique, since Joyce had referred to Eliot only as "Your friend Mr. Eliot." But Joyce *was* convinced that the world ought to support him. Eliot wrote Quinn that he had read part of *Ulysses* in manuscript and found it truly magnificent, and he and Harriet Weaver both tried to persuade the

Woolfs to publish it at Hogarth Press. The holiday, spent walking and biking about the French countryside, restored Eliot enough to return to work.

The Eliots had finally managed to rent a better apartment at 9 Clarence Gate Gardens, a large Victorian building near Regent's Park. They lived there for the next ten years, sharing their home with a cat or two who were very much part of the family and were eventually portrayed in *Old Possum's Book of Practical Cats*.

In December 1920 Eliot's first collection of critical essays, *The Sacred Wood*, came out in both England and America, dedicated to Eliot's father. This little book, which Eliot typically deprecated, had mixed reviews, but is still in print. Together with *The Waste Land*, it was *The Sacred Wood* that made Eliot's name.

In *The Sacred Wood* Eliot made the most influential of his poetic and philosophic proclamations. He affirmed his lifelong intellectual position as a "reactionary radical," like G. K. Chesterton, by urging continuity with one's roots but still affirming the need to "redeem the time."

Eliot told his readers the plan he meant to follow as a poet-critic; then in *The Waste Land*, he showed them how to do it. By accomplishing this feat, Eliot so captured the imagination of his contemporaries that he could later command attention for his Christian message. There was more than a touch of the young Saul (later the apostle Paul) in the Eliot of *The Sacred Wood*: both were serious-minded, highly intelligent, and zealous for a cause that they later came to see in an entirely new light. If C. S. Lewis became, in the words of Chad Walsh, the "apostle to the skeptics," then Eliot became the "apostle to the intellectuals." The paradox of Eliot's career was the fact that, within five years of making these literary pronouncements, which were to be used by all serious critics to discuss modern literature, Eliot had reversed himself to become a public spokesman for morality in art.

Today it is also evident that Eliot, speaking here as the stern young "classical" critic who called for literature to move away from the Romantic cult of sincerity and amateurish artlessness, was a late-blooming Romantic like Joyce and Kafka. Like Arnold and Emerson, these twentieth-century writers relied heavily on themselves in their quest for a way to structure the modern world.

Eliot began by talking about his poetic predecessors in literary criticism. First he talked about Matthew Arnold, whom he had made fun of in "Cousin Nancy" as one of the twin guardians (with Emerson) of manners and morés in Boston. Now Eliot apologized to Arnold, who had tried to deal with the subjective approach of the Romantics, a job that Eliot's generation needed to do again. But Eliot scolded Arnold for making the mistake of dropping pure criticism to become a politician, or commentator on the social scene—a job done better by an editorial writer. Eliot declared that it was always a temptation for a man interested in ideas to put literature in the corner until he cleaned up the country. He then praised (or damned) H. G. Wells and G. K. Chesterton for doing this so well that they showed this was the work they should be doing.

Eliot attacked the Romantics' disorder, vagueness, and social agendas, as well as their Impressionistic techniques. He used terms like those used by the young Chesterton, who had attacked the Impressionists' use of faint, wavy lines instead of strong, sharp strokes. The best critic was an artist who looked at the work from the craftsman's point of view, but the perfect critic only elucidated the work, letting readers judge for themselves. Critics should stick to criticizing, making use of influential "little magazines" to exchange ideas with their peers. Their task was to preserve what is good in the tradition, trying to view both today's work and the work of the past the same way.

Eliot's critical heroes now were the unemotional Aristotle, the man of universal intelligence; Dr. Samuel Johnson (a devout Christian and Chestertonian hero); and, most important, Dante, whom Eliot declared had a saner approach to the mystery of life than Shakespeare. Eliot said that the two forms of "sensibility"—criticism and creation—were complementary, so the poet and the critic should be the same person.

The single most famous essay in *The Sacred Wood* was "Tradition and the Individual Talent." Eliot began it by turning the discussion of tradition upside down, declaring that the English seldom spoke of tradition except to deplore its absence or to blame someone for being too traditional. The English also pretended that only the places where a poet's work was like everyone else's showed his genius.

Eliot disagreed, and very much as Chesterton had suggested a few years earlier in *The Victorian Age in Literature*, said that we should not "disenfranchise our ancestors" or assume that an artist is an individual

alone, because he must be understood in relation to his age. As Dorothy
L. Sayers later said in "Towards a Christian Aesthetic," one poet's work
depended on and was enriched by the work of others.

But today's poets could not just inherit tradition; they had to obtain
it by great labor, developing their historical understanding that all
literature has a "simultaneous existence and composes a simultaneous
order." That historical sense of the timeless and the temporal together
made a writer "traditional," but he must also know his own place in
time. Charles Williams would say that an artist and his work must "coinhere" in time and eternity.

Eliot went on to point out, in an argument like that of G. K. Chesterton five years later in *The Everlasting Man*, that a poet was judged not
only by the present but by the past. Art never progressed; only its
materials changed. Art did not leave behind either Shakespeare or the
drawings of the cavemen. When people insisted that dead writers were
unimportant because we know so much more than they did, Eliot replied
that as artists, they must understand that those very writers were what
they knew. Forgotten or not, we have built our work on theirs.

Eliot, however, was interested only in the poem itself, not in the
writer or his life. The best poetry was created by the poet's condensing
his emotions, words, and ideas in his own mind, then recreating them
in an objective, impersonal experience, rather than describing them or
reacting to them as if writing a diary or a letter to a friend. Eliot's statements were to became the basis for the "New Criticism," which wanted
to avoid C. S. Lewis's "personal heresy," in which the poet's state of
mind was used to explain the poem.

In another essay in *The Sacred Wood* called "The Possibility of a
Poetic Drama," Eliot foreshadowed his own literary agenda. Many
poets, he claimed, wanted to write for the stage because a poetic drama
provided the most permanent dramatic form, one that could show
more varieties of society than any other. Poetic drama allowed the artist to write for more groups than for the small group who wanted
"poetry"; such an artist could imitate the Elizabethans by writing for the
large public who want entertainment. But writing poetic drama
depended upon the temper of the times.

The Sacred Wood ended with essays on individual dramatists like
Shakespeare, Marlowe, Massinger, and Jonson, and then with an

important essay on Dante in which Eliot described Dante as a "philosopher poet." A philosopher poet was one who was able to deal with ideas in poetry. Because Dante's philosophy was basic to his world view, *The Divine Comedy* had both form and structure. Dante's poetic greatness lay in the fact that his individual verses were incomprehensible without understanding the whole poem.

The Sacred Wood appeared at just the right moment. The postwar literary generation was looking for a new sense of order and certainty which they found lacking in society. Eliot's ideas formed a "new whole" that reaffirmed literature's usefulness as a way of organizing private experience.

Eliot was again suffering from his form of "writer's block," an inability to write poetry when he was under pressure. Conrad Aiken consulted a psychiatrist friend who said that Eliot couldn't write because he had to write perfectly; in other words, "he thinks he's God." Aiken repeated this to Eliot, making Eliot extremely angry at this invasion of his privacy and—possibly— appalled at the blasphemy.

During the fall of 1920 Vivien was in very bad health. Her father had been seriously ill and she and Eliot had helped nurse him. Then she began to suffer a number of nervous physical problems. Eliot cared for her, carried on with his job at the bank, wrote more reviews, and tinkered with parts of *The Waste Land*. Still, Vivien's emotional dependence on him, together with her health problems, demanded energy he did not have to spare. This aspect of their lives together was as significant in their deteriorating marriage as their sexual relationship.

Eliot had begun to contribute to *The Dial*, edited by his Harvard friend Scofield Thayer, who had introduced the Eliots. Eliot wrote several pieces for Thayer on London music-hall performers, in which he said he wanted to capture for serious poetic drama their stylized forms and large audiences.

Having lived in England for five years, Eliot felt he was less of an onlooker at English life. The underlying problems of the postwar world became very obvious as unemployment rose, despite the eight million dead. Old beliefs seemed undermined by Freud, Marx, and the modern "sciences" of anthropology and sociology. Politically, revolution seemed to be in the air. All these problems were being ignored by Lloyd George's coalition government, which had swept into office on

Armistice euphoria. Like many of his contemporaries, Eliot saw the political and economic situation as an example of the inefficiency of democracy; through it demagogues found opportunity to gain power for personal greed. To many the only alternative seemed to be state control, either fascist or socialist.

Many of the upper-middle-class, educated Englishmen whom Eliot knew were socialists, ready to tell ordinary people what was good for them, but still preserved a class oligarchy in their educational and social institutions. If outwardly Eliot became more English than the English, inwardly he never completely gave up the ideal of American-style democracy or lost the Puritan sense of moral purpose and personal responsibility that demanded a crucial role for the individual.

In the summer of 1921, after much urging on his part, Eliot's widowed mother arrived for a visit together with his sister Marian and his brother Henry. At seventy-seven, Charlotte Eliot greatly surprised Eliot with her energy. Whenever Eliot is accused of being afraid of women, it ought to be remembered that the women whose company he appreciated were people like his mother and sisters: forthright, determined, educated, busy about the world, and accustomed to taking care of their men instead of being taken care of. (Eliot's second wife was an English version of an Eliot woman.)

Much as Eliot wished to see his family, these visitors from America did not help the Eliots' marriage either. Eliot's mother blamed Vivien for Eliot's staying in England instead of returning to America, where he "belonged." Vivien Eliot was frightened by her mother-in-law and spent part of the visit away in a country cottage. Nonetheless, the visit was a success. With a great deal of nervous effort, Eliot managed to keep everyone reasonably content, and his mother enjoyed sightseeing and meeting "important people" like Lady Ottoline Morrell. Although Henry always expressed the belief that one day Eliot would "come home," their visit helped Eliot see how far removed he was from America. He knew his literary career could not succeed as well there.

In the midst of the family visit Eliot was trying to set up an English version of *The Dial*. Another little magazine, it was to be backed financially by Lady Rothermere. A member of the newspaper family who almost controlled Fleet Street, she may have wanted a paper of her own to give her status in the literary world. At one point Vivien Eliot came back from the country to help Eliot with the negotiations. As a bank employee, Eliot could not earn an outside salary, so as editor of the new publication, *The Criterion*, he would be paid only for his own articles.

As he worked with the pieces of *The Waste Land* during 1921, Eliot was also reading and writing about the seventeenth-century's metaphysical poets, as well as about primitive religions in Sir James Frazer's *The Golden Bough*, Jessie L. Weston's book on the Grail legend, *From Ritual to Romance*, and Freud's *Totem and Taboo*. Those books challenged the nineteenth-century idea of Western progress and stressed the common mythic foundation of all cultures, past and present, Western and non-Western.

Eliot had read James Joyce's *Ulysses* in manuscript, admiring his "mythic method" of giving shape and significance to the anarchy of modern history. He had even attended séances organized by his patron Lady Rothermere. All these things found their way into his poem. But by September, when his family left, Eliot was totally worn out. Vivien made him see a nerve specialist who insisted he take three months off to be by himself and do absolutely nothing, so Eliot was obliged to ask for a three months' leave from Lloyds.

He went first to Margate, escorted by Vivien, who then left him alone. That month Eliot composed "The Fire Sermon" part of *The Waste Land* (his hotel bill was found attached to that part of the manuscript). Eliot next proposed to drop Vivien off to visit the Pounds in Paris. She would then go to a sanatorium while he went to stay alone in a cottage near Monte Carlo. He wrote a friend asking if he could take care of their small cat, a very good mouser.

But, acting on advice from several people, that November Eliot instead went to see a pre-Freudian Swiss psychiatrist at Lausanne. His treatment helped Eliot to relax and not worry so much. As a fascinating result, Eliot wrote the final, somewhat positive, segment of *The Waste Land* called "What the Thunder Said." A compulsive and meticulous rewriter, Eliot reported that he made fewer changes in that section than in any other of his poems.

Eliot returned to Paris in December 1921 to rejoin Vivien and return to England—and to leave his new poem with Pound for criticism and editing. After reading the manuscript of *The Waste Land*, Pound wrote John Quinn in New York that Eliot's poem was "about enough to make the rest of us shut up shop," although Pound characteristically added that he wasn't going to do that.

This was the last time Pound edited Eliot's poetry. Evidence from the manuscript, published after its rediscovery in 1971, shows that Pound made major alterations, chiefly by cutting the poem and by removing "connecting passages." That made its contrasts more vivid and its effects more dramatic; in a sense it was Pound who made *The Waste Land* the paradigm of Modernist poetry.

Eliot let Pound take charge, even at the risk of having the poem transformed into something quite different from his original intentions. Long afterward he told a *Paris Review* interviewer that before Pound worked on the poem it was "just as structureless, only in a more futile way."

The result of their combined work was the "poem of the century." Eliot later repudiated the idea that he was making any sort of manifesto, insisting that the poem was only "a personal grouse." He also admitted that a poem can mean different things to its readers than to its author. Nonetheless, Eliot was marked as the writer of *The Waste Land* for the rest of his life.

Critical attention has veered back and forth between *The Waste Land* as public statement and as personal confession. In general, critics and public first took the viewpoint that the poem was a public message which described the dreary modern world with its broken center; its title became part of the language used to describe that period.

Others said that there was no unity of vision except in the "unified response" of the reader who creates the poem's order. Or they saw the contrasts as representing accurate reporting, interpreted only by the poem's suggestion of unity between the contrasting images. Later critics began to use the poem to search for fragments of Eliot's personal life, a pursuit intensified by the belated discovery of the original manuscript.

While interpretations of the poem grew, its images spoke directly to younger postwar writers. In *The Great Gatsby*, Scott Fitzgerald has a miniature waste land between West Egg and New York. Ernest Hemingway's hero in *The Sun Also Rises* is impotent, representative of "the Lost Generation." In Evelyn Waugh's *Brideshead Revisited* his aesthetic undergraduate Anthony Blanche recited *The Waste Land* from a balcony to Oxford students on their way to row on the river. Waugh, using a line from Eliot, also called an earlier comic novel *A Handful of Dust*.

By the '30s, influenced by the fact of Eliot's conversion, critics insisted that the poem showed a passage or progression, which was completed by an affirmation of religious belief disguised in modern symbols. This reading of religion back into Eliot's preconversion life was intensified by critics after they had seen the original manuscript of *The Waste Land*. They insist that the poem started as a "typical" Eliot poem about his vocation to a religious life, but since Pound neither understood nor accepted this purpose, he changed the poem into a statement on contemporary culture.

Current student guides to the poem try to combine all of these approaches, but still insist that *The Waste Land* is not a personal document but a study of civilization. That broad approach helps the ordinary reader understand that in the poem Eliot, with the help of Pound, objectified his own response to the world so effectively that his personal hell became the compelling portrait of the spirit of an age.

The Waste Land portrays failed civilization, or St. Augustine's "earthly city," doomed by its sterility and loss of spiritual power. There is little suggestion in the poem of any vision of the "city of God." But Eliot's use of historic moments of symbolic drama gave the poem a shape and significance that pointed beyond the futility of the modern world to a new form, or order.

The poem can be read as a narrative with philosophical overtones, much like Virgil's *Aeneid* or Dante's *Divine Comedy*. Eliot used "moments" from old stories to provide a "plot"; the fragments Eliot shored against his ruins were the words of past poets. At the poem's heart lay the legend of the Grail, a potent myth for other twentieth-century Christians like Charles Williams, for whom it also symbolized a spiritual quest. Moving away from a timid J. Alfred Prufrock who did not dare to ask the overwhelming question, Eliot began to question the horror and ask to be healed.

Eliot's personal inclination may have always been toward what Charles Williams called the Negative Way; his admiration of Buddhism and Indian religions suggest that. But not all Christian saints have been martyrs like Savonarola. The seventeenth century was filled with Puritan "saints" who practiced self-examination, but worked out their salvation in the world, hoping to transform the time. Like G. K. Chesterton before him and C. S. Lewis shortly afterward, Eliot was slowly moving away from a bright adolescent's solipsistic, meaningless world view, just as he was discovering that his ethical upbringing, which had taught him to substitute good works for grace, did not help him deal with his sense of sin.

By January 1922 Eliot was back at his desk in the bank while he, Pound, and Quinn tried to market the poem to the best advantage. As a result of Quinn's help both in England and America, Eliot wrote him that he wanted to give him the original manuscript. When Quinn wrote back, offering to pay for it, Eliot insisted that it must be a gift.

The unexpected result of Eliot's generosity was that when Quinn died in 1924, the manuscript of *The Waste Land* disappeared. In the 1950s his niece found it among her uncle's papers and sold it to the Berg Collection of the New York City Library without telling either Pound or Eliot. The Berg curator also never told Eliot; so it was not until after Eliot's death that Mrs. Eliot learned that the Berg Collection had the manuscript. With the help of Pound she was able to prepare it for publication in 1971.

The original manuscript revealed that Eliot and his wife Vivien had worked together on the poem section by section. Her marginal comments also showed that the poem was not a deliberately autobiographical description of their relationship, but that Eliot had paid serious attention to her opinions. It did not demonstrate that Vivien Eliot had really written the poem, as some critics have suggested.

Rediscovery of the manuscript also showed that Ezra Pound had done a drastic amount of cutting, which did change the effect of the work. By deleting whole sections (like "Gerontion") that were closer in spirit to Eliot's earlier poems, Pound had turned *The Waste Land* into a Modernist masterpiece, ready to stand beside Picasso's *Les Demoiselles d'Avignon*, Stravinsky's *The Rite of Spring*, and Joyce's *Ulysses*.

Pound unquestionably had an excellent ear. He improved individual lines, as well as excised weak ones. Well read in the intellectual sources used by Eliot, Pound, in some respects, made the perfect editor. Without his work, the poem probably would not have made such a splash.

In October 1922 *The Waste Land* was published in America and England. In the United States Scofield Thayer published it in *The Dial* and in England it appeared in the first issue of Eliot's *Criterion*. The book version was published in New York on December 15. It also had Eliot's notes, chiefly to make it long enough for a book. Later, Eliot said he was sorry he had sent so many critics searching for Tarot cards, Grail legends, and vegetable religious ceremonies.

The notes are useful, however, for the serious reader because they provide clues to Eliot's sources and interests. They show that in addition to the trendy sociological and anthropological sources like Frazer and Weston, Eliot also had used personal sources of tradition, like the Bible, seventeenth-century dramatists and poets, Greek myths, St. Augustine, the Buddha, Shakespeare, and Dante, who were all guides leading him to Christianity.

CHAPTER SIX

The Turning
1922 - 1930

*H*AVING ROCKETED INTO FAME ON THE STRENGTH OF *The Waste Land*, Eliot found himself almost trapped by its popularity in the literary world. He had written to his mother, who had recently moved east to live near her other children, that much of his life was in the poem, and it made him happy when she admired it. But Eliot was increasingly distressed by the fact that he was identified both with the poem and with critics' interpretations of it, when he wanted to get to work on something else.

Vivien continued to be in ill health much of the time, and Eliot was continually exhausted by working, editing *The Criterion*, and trying to write something new. He wrote to John Quinn that largely because of her he had turned down the prestigious but financially insecure job as editor of the old *Liberal Nation*. Vivien became hysterical if Eliot suggested quitting the bank job, which paid her medical bills, and guaranteed her a pension if he died. Meanwhile Eliot was trying to put any extra money he earned from writing into a special account against the day when he could leave the bank. Quinn started giving Eliot four hundred dollars a year, but he died suddenly in 1924.

Everyone now took it for granted that Vivien was a chronic invalid. Pound again started a "save Eliot" fund, embarrassing Eliot and endangering his bank job when the scheme became public. In 1925 Henry, Eliot's older brother about to be married at the age of forty-six, wrote a candid letter to Harriet Monroe at *Poetry*, telling her that his brother had a chronically sick wife which made creative work very difficult. Henry then sent a small contribution to *Poetry* (to which he subscribed) in spite of his own "ample field for assisting poetry" in his own family.

As Vivien's health and mental stability worsened, Eliot was not able to keep on nursing her or her artistic potential at his own expense. He consulted Leonard Woolf, who had taken charge of his wife Virginia's schedule, about how to ration Vivien's work. Eliot and his wife were naive in thinking that their contemporaries would not gossip about them when their private lives made such "good copy," and Eliot's growing stature in the literary world was making his rivals jealous. Ironically, chief among those whose testimony is often treated as gospel truth was Virginia Woolf. Her letters and diaries have made her a main source for many commentators, who ignore the fact that in personal relationships Woolf was unstable and often malicious.

Friends and self-described "disciples" like Herbert Read, who often stayed with the Eliots if he was too late to catch a train home to Beaconsfield, were sad at the sight of the deteriorating marriage. But such friends rarely spoke about the situation to Eliot, who also did not often bring it up. Obviously his fame intensified this diffidence.

From its beginning, Eliot's ambition was to make *The Criterion* reflect "the living mind of Europe," not just England, despite his increasing identification with that country and its literature. He hoped to make it a meeting place for all writers concerned with the disinterested examination of ideas, although Pound called Eliot's idea that the greatest poets had been concerned with moral values "bunkum." What these two poets never lost was their mutual conviction that literary criticism must be done by those who wrote the literature. As has been noted, however, after the publication of *The Waste Land* their relationship became less close.

Eliot did not use his little magazine to sell a party platform or create a school of thought, but managed to fill *The Criterion* with a remarkable group of international writers, many of whom disagreed with his literary, religious, or social agendas. Together with Pound, whose *Cantos* Eliot published whenever Pound gave him one, *The Criterion's* most famous contributors were Marcel Proust, Jean Cocteau, Jacques Maritain, Virginia Woolf, Wyndham Lewis, James Joyce, Aldous Huxley, and younger poets like W. H. Auden and Stephen Spender.

Being editor meant that Eliot now lunched with contributors, often established authors like Hugh Walpole, and met others like Gertrude Stein. *The Criterion* survived for seventeen years. Its price was high, and its circulation never more than a thousand, yet between the wars it made its editor the most important arbiter of modern literature.

The Criterion reflected the development of Eliot's ideas and beliefs. Even before the publication of *The Waste Land* he had begun to move away from the Metaphysical poets and John Donne to study Dante and St. Thomas Aquinas as well as other medieval mystics. Now, under the influence of French philosophers like Etienne Gilson and Jacques Maritain, he became better acquainted with modern Thomism, which seemed to contain the things needed to recreate Europe.

At the same time, what Eliot as a writer now wanted to create was a new kind of drama that would speak directly to the modern urban world. He had always liked the theater, and he felt that drama was the ideal medium for poetry and the best way to make poetry socially useful.

Ironically, Pound agreed, saying that drama was "didactic." The major cuts Pound had made in *The Waste Land* had taken out a number of Eliot's "different voices," destroying the dramatic structure of the original poem. He also made it less evident that Eliot's "Sweeney Agonistes" was related to it.

Always a willing and earnest student, Eliot consulted Georgian novelist and playwright Arnold Bennett, who had theatrical expertise and command of a wide audience. Eliot told Bennett that he wanted to go beyond the nineteenth century's "realistic" drama to create a play that was "self-consistent" but was an abstraction or simplification of real life. He wanted to create a drama that combined classical Greek, Elizabethan, and Jacobean drama, as well as his favorite music hall routines and Stravinsky ballets like *The Rite of Spring*.

His struggle to produce such a work, for which he had no model, was difficult, and the play was never completed. It was published in two parts as an unfinished poetic drama called *Sweeney Agonistes* between 1925 and 1927. Loosely based on the comedies of Aristophanes, its captions were from Aeschylus' *Oresteia* and the Christian mystic St. John of the Cross. The one dramatizes the hero's haunting by the Furies, the other, the soul's need to divest itself of the love of created beings. Those themes were to reappear in Eliot's other quite different dramas, *Murder in the Cathedral* and *The Family Reunion*.

In the play Sweeney offers to take his girlfriend Doris off to the South Seas, where he threatens to eat her. The idea of escaping there had been a part of Eliot's imagination ever since he read Robert Louis Stevenson's stories and admired Gauguin's paintings. The music-hall pantomines he enjoyed also featured South Sea island skits. (Chesterton had used the escape motif in a different way in *Orthodoxy*, where, by adventuring to the South Seas, he found himself to be at home.) In Eliot's unfinished drama, Sweeney and Doris stay at home, arguing about who is knocking at their door—the landlord or God.

The Woolfs had published *The Waste Land* in book form in 1923. Virginia Woolf set the poem in type herself, becoming familiar enough with it that echoes appeared in her own writing. The Woolfs considered themselves to be Eliot's English publishers, and his work added luster to Hogarth Press. At their request in 1924, Eliot gave them three of his *Times Literary Supplement* essays on Dryden, Marvell, and the Metaphysical poets. The Hogarth Press published them with the title *Homage to John Dryden*.

In those essays Eliot once again turned conventional wisdom upside down by asserting that the Metaphysical Poets were not a quaint group who wrote obscurely, but represented the time before Milton and Dryden began to "dissociate sensibility." After them, poets separated their feelings from their ideas, and instead of describing their experiences, reflected on them in poetic language.

By contrast, the poet Andrew Marvell, who came before the "dissociation," reflects the traditional European way of life that was a product of Latin civilization. Eliot preferred Marvell to John Milton because Marvell represented the larger group of English Puritans, who chose to be ruled by their peers, not a Stuart king. It was these men who were not extremists and who reflected the real spirit of their age. In another essay he defended Dryden from the nineteenth-century charge that he did not write about "poetic" subjects, insisting that without reading Dryden you cannot understand Wordsworth, Keats, or Shelley.

The summer of 1924 Eliot's mother again came to visit, but Vivien was spending more and more time isolated in the country, nursing herself. When she felt up to it she worked on *The Criterion*, and Eliot published some of her writings there. Although most observers believed that Vivien always worshiped Eliot, in one of her *Criterion* sketches a character complained that her husband had worked so hard to conquer all literary worlds that he failed to do much writing himself. It was close to the truth, since Eliot was having one of his dry spells.

The Criterion continued to use up most of Eliot's free time and energy. By the mid '20s, Eliot had begun meeting once a week at The Grove in Knightsbridge with some of *The Criterion* contributors, supporters, and other interested writers. But actual *Criterion* meetings took place about once a month at night in a restaurant in Soho. Those gatherings were lively and stimulating evenings that showed Eliot at his most relaxed and amusing, but they did not help him "get out the paper." Eliot did most of that work himself, with the help of a part-time secretary. Marketing, publishing, and business affairs were handled by Richard Cobden-Sanderson, who reported back to their angel, Lady Rothermere.

Sometime in 1923 Cobden-Sanderson, whose parties Eliot often attended, introduced Eliot to a fellow American, William Force Stead. Stead had been born in Washington, D.C., came to England as a young diplomat, but had resigned to be ordained in the Church of England. He now served as chaplain of Worcester College, Oxford, but he also wrote and published poetry. They became friends and correspondents. Stead and Eliot talked about the writings of seventeenth-century Anglican divines, especially Bishop Lancelot Andrewes, whom they both admired.

Andrewes's devotional prayers had been published after he died, but it was Eliot who showed the world that Andrewes was also a significant preacher. Following in the footsteps of the Elizabethan "Judicious" Hooker, Bishop Andrewes's emotions were controlled by his intellect.

Eliot found he felt more sympathy for the cool, cultivated "medieval temper" of Andrewes than for John Donne's flashing brilliance.

In Richard Hooker and his successors, Anglican bishops Andrewes and Bramhall, Eliot found a breadth of culture that had kept the medieval tradition and combined it with Renaissance learning to make them true Europeans, as well as founders of a national church. In Andrewes's writings, Eliot also discovered "orthodox" Christianity, especially the doctrine of the incarnation of Christ.

Almost ten years earlier, in his extension lectures Eliot had talked about the social value of the church, which he called "classicism." By classicism, here Eliot meant a structured way of worship and devotional living. Those lunch hours spent in Wren churches had impressed him not only with their beauty, but with their worshipers, whom he discovered on their knees (an Eliot aunt had once said that no Eliot would ever assume such a humiliating attitude).

Some of Eliot's early poetry had described a solitary Puritan ascetic, looking for "mystical moments of vision;" some poems had been satirical about organized religion; some had made use in a Modernist way of Christian myths. But by now there were many personal reasons why Eliot's responsibilities and ambitions made a retreat into the *via negativa* of contemplation unlikely.

Through Andrewes and others, Eliot became aware of the church as a traditional institution, which stood for a middle ground between skepticism and isolation. Just as Chesterton had realized that the roots of his family's Liberal faith came from the church, Eliot now began to understand that orthodox Christianity was the ground on which the civilization he wanted to preserve was built.

Unlike Roman Catholicism, which had a strange and foreign feel, the Church of England had powerful associations because of his English roots and its magnificent language. The writings of Hooker and Andrewes had designed and built the intellectual structure of the English church much as St. Thomas Aquinas' philosophy had defined the thirteenth century and made a Dante possible. Andrewes in particular had a spiritual discipline which fitted Eliot's own lifelong search for a rule to live by. So for Eliot, seeking self-control as well as the assurance of grace and pardon, the Church of England represented a true middle ground. Ignoring his Puritan heritage, he added that "the *via media* is of all ways the most difficult to follow."

Eliot's public commitment to Christianity was to be based on a tension between his intellect and his emotions that paralleled the church as a *via media*. Its personal, emotional basis was reflected in his poetry, but his criticism showed that his intellect was converted as well. No matter how much Eliot was drawn to church ritual and liturgy both as discipline and experience, like Chesterton, Sayers, and C. S. Lewis, he always insisted that his conversion to orthodoxy was motivated by reason.

Contrary to the opinion of many critics, Eliot did not invent his own version of Christianity or ignore traditional credal affirmations to practice a kind of Modernist Christian "improvisation." Once he had joined the church, Eliot publicly practiced the faith preserved by Christendom throughout the ages, while privately struggling with the depression and skepticism that were part of his birthright as a modern man.

Paradoxically, however, it was in 1925, while he was studying Andrewes and becoming closer acquainted with the Church of England, that Eliot published *The Hollow Men*. This is the poem of his which best expresses the doom of the modern "damned." Ten years later, in his last BBC broadcast, Chesterton took public exception to its despair by mocking the poem's famous closing with the lines: "They may end with a whimper/But we shall end with a bang." Chesterton was not reacting against Eliot personally, but against the spirit of the times which had seized this poem as its watchword.

Unlike the more complicated and cinemagraphic *The Waste Land*, *The Hollow Men* has simple, direct images and repetitions that are close to modern speech. Its ambiguous refrains from the Lord's Prayer, however, have allowed some critics to call it "Christian." For most of Eliot's contemporaries the poem expressed the horrors of the age of anxiety. In Dorothy L. Sayers's *Busman's Honeymoon*, for example, in the chapter called "Prickly Pear," Lord Peter Wimsey had a nightmare about World War I "responsibility," in which a group of uniformed men, hanged and chained together, march on broken feet across a prickly desert.

Often called Eliot's version of Dante's *Hell*, or a mini- *The Waste Land*, *The Hollow Men* marks the point where a great change, or

turning, occurred in Eliot's life. After it happened, it was noted by all
his contemporaries and was reflected in his poetry and prose. Herbert
Read, who called himself "romantic and agnostic," called *The Hollow
Men* the most confessional of Eliot's poems, but the last of his "pure"
poetry before Eliot began to "moralize." Conrad Aiken greatly admired
The Hollow Men and wrote Eliot to praise it. In reply he received a
peculiar clipping about mucus, blood, and pus, a sign of Eliot's frantic
preoccupation with Vivien's worsening illnesses and his own despair.
Aiken felt that Eliot was to desert the modern world to retreat into
medievalism.

In 1925 Eliot made an important career change. He left the bank to
become a director or editor of the newly established publishing firm of
Faber & Gwyer, which soon became Faber & Faber. He was to work
there the rest of his life, just as Charles Williams worked at Oxford
University Press.

Eliot had been introduced to Geoffrey Faber as someone whose
poetic reputation would help the new firm attract younger writers. He
was also by now an experienced editor and businessman. Eliot filled
those roles admirably and, according to his friend and associate Frank
Morley, was always a "willing workhorse."

One of his talents was writing clever jacket blurbs. He was also ex-
ceptionally good at dealing with the firm's more difficult clients. Many
years later in New York Eliot put his young editor Roger Giroux at ease
by asking if he had "much author trouble." He always showed complete
loyalty to the firm, never pushing himself or his own enthusiasms (except perhaps for publishing Ezra Pound). Because he did not trade on
his influence, it grew.

A case in point was *The Criterion*. When Lady Rothermere grew dis-
enchanted with patronizing the arts and stopped subsidizing it, the
magazine was saved by its other subscribers. Then in 1927 it was taken
over by Faber & Faber and rechristened *The New Criterion*. Eliot continued to edit it (for nothing) until he closed it down in 1939 on the brink
of war.

Faber & Faber also began to publish Eliot's own works, a wonderful
"security" for a born worrier. Eliot remained appreciative all his life. In
return, he formed the taste of a generation and "made" Faber & Faber
by publishing most of the best-known poets of the twentieth century.

The Woolfs, who had published his earlier work, felt that Eliot had been disloyal. But their accusation that Bloomsbury had "made" Eliot rang hollow. By the late '20s the anecdotes Bloomsbury liked to tell about Eliot when he first arrived in London seemed unbelievable to the younger generation of writers, who greatly revered him as *the* poet-critic of their times.

Looking back in 1939, Eliot wrote in *The Criterion* that 1926 had been the year when the war finally ended and the postwar world was born. Literature written before that date belonged to the "last of the old world." In many ways Eliot was correct that 1926 was a watershed. It was the year of the General Strike, while the Liberal Party, the middle ground or *via media* of English politics, was destroyed for good. It was replaced by a duel between the left and the right, who in England were Labour and the Conservatives. In much the same way the growing strength of fascism and communism was destroying representative government abroad. Reflecting on this sober scene, Chesterton, who had recently reorganized his small paper as *G. K.'s Weekly*, rewrote and published his novel, *The Return of Don Quixote*. It was a melancholy vision of an England needing to be redeemed by a return to her spiritual roots.

Eliot also sought to redeem the time by a discussion in *The Criterion* of England's heritage of freedom, order, and justice. He located these qualities in the Crown, the unwritten constitution, and the Common Law. He sought to establish a middle ground like Chesterton's Liberalism. But Eliot's political outlook was also colored by his American background of New England federalism and Middle Western republicanism, both based on the tradition of a country founded on a creed.

Unlike their English forebears, whose system was built on a long history of separate documents and common usage, from the time of the Mayflower Compact to the Declaration of Independence, Americans had taken for granted a written social contract that was the final word. Such a document was their justification for government in the way that the Bible was their basis for belief. There was, therefore, a subtly un-English quality to Eliot's ultimate espousal of hierarchical society. His opinions about what was useful and workable also changed over time, as he reminded his listeners at Leeds in 1961.

It was, however, decidedly in response to the growing religious fervor of the ideologies of left and right that, during 1926, Eliot made up his mind to become a British citizen and to join the Church of England. (Since the Church of England is an established church, closely tied to the Crown, Eliot regarded the two as a single step.)

The times made Eliot feel a need to stand up and be counted. Like Chesterton's decision in 1922 to become a Roman Catholic, the public nature of these commitments was intentional. Eliot was using them to act out in his own life the social and ethical concerns his little magazine discussed.

Instead of "medievalism" and "monasticism," Eliot was learning what made up the Anglican tradition. The church taught that instead of being a depraved sinner unless he saw the light, as a child of God and a member of the church, he would grow in grace. Its tradition said that there were many means to salvation beside studying the Bible and preaching, principally the faithful practice of the sacraments and the discipline of common, or community, prayer. There was merit in human reason and public authority, and the church made a prudent distinction between the invisible church of the saved and the visible church of the realm.

But in spite of the great comfort and long-lasting effect his decisions had on Eliot's life, he would not have made either commitment unless it represented a deep personal conviction. Neither decision was easy. His American family would be upset by the first and his non-religious wife by the second.

Vivien's attitude was particularly important to their relationship because by now Eliot was beginning to discuss with close friends and his family the possibility of a separation. It was obvious to everyone that Vivien and he did one another harm. But Eliot also knew that the very idea of a separation would make Vivien's condition worse and further, the Church of England did not recognize divorce.

Eliot gave his public some indication how his ideas were changing. Early in 1926 he gave the Clark Lectures at Cambridge University. His literary reputation was being nurtured there by his friend and admirer, Professor I. A. Richards of Magdalene College. Eliot came to stay with the Richardses, wearing a knapsack and bringing a large, new *Book of Common Prayer*. He asked his dumbfounded (and ill-informed) hosts about the services at the Cambridge churches. Eliot was trying to discover which church would have an Anglo-Catholic, or "High Church" service of Holy Communion. At that time, most Anglican churches had Holy Communion only at Early Church. As a result, people like Dorothy L. Sayers, who disliked sermons, and C. S. Lewis, who did not care for music, usually went, like Eliot, to Early Church.

To prepare for his Clark lectures, Eliot had been studying Neo-Thomists like Jacques Maritain in relation to his topic, which was the seventeenth-century's Metaphysical poets. Maritain was seeking to reacquaint the twentieth century with St. Thomas Aquinas and its historic Christian roots. By reinterpreting Aristotle, St. Thomas had given the thirteenth century an intellectually unified European culture which made Dante possible. In his lectures on the Metaphysical Poets, Eliot now discussed how the unity and order of Aquinas's day had been lost and tried to suggest how to reestablish it in the modern world.

During 1926 Eliot also paid his mother a lovely compliment. Through his efforts, her long poem *Savonarola* was published with a carefully impersonal introduction written by her poet son. (On several occasions Eliot was accused of being too "impersonal" in his comments. One was in this introduction, another in his obituary of Virginia Woolf. Both times he was behaving—in his eyes—properly and impartially, as became a critic whose opinion counted, rather than being sentimental as a son or friend.)

That March the Eliots moved into a better apartment near Sloane Square in Chelsea. But Vivien's health and spirits continued to fluctuate wildly, and she spent most of her time in clinics abroad. On one occasion they were both traveling in Europe with Vivien's brother Maurice and his wife. During a visit to St. Peter's in Rome, Eliot embarrassed the others by falling to his knees in front of Michelangelo's *Pieta*. Any Christian who has felt an impulse to piety instead of aesthetic appreciation when visiting a famous church can understand Eliot's action. But falling to his knees in front of the statue of Dante at Sante Croce in Florence would have been more socially acceptable.

That June at a sanatorium near Geneva, Switzerland, the Eliots met another patient named Gordon George (who wrote under the name of Roger Sencourt). George had grown up in New Zealand and gone to St. John College, Oxford. George was an ardent member of the Anglo-Catholic wing of the Church of England. He was also passionately committed to entente between Rome and Canterbury. George introduced Eliot to the elderly Lord Halifax, the leading Anglo-Catholic layman in the Church of England, and to Francis Underhill, the priest who became Bishop of Bath and Wells.

Lord Halifax was head of the Church Union. It was one of the outgrowths of the nineteenth-century Oxford Movement, which had been led by Keble, Pusey, and Newman (who later became a Roman Catholic). The Oxford Movement emphasized the Anglican Church's historical roots in pre-Reformation England. It reestablished catholic worship that emphasized the importance of the sacraments, the role of bishops in the apostolic succession, and an Augustinian justification by faith instead of good works. The Oxford Movement had also given rise to a devout social activist group, the Christian Social Union, that was instrumental in Chesterton's becoming an orthodox Christian.

Most Anglo-Catholics believe that their branch of Christendom has as much apostolic validity as the Church of Rome. Like Eliot's Puritan ancestors, the Anglo-Catholics wanted to "purify" church usage, not return to one universal church. At the same time, like G. K Chesterton, Eliot had come to dislike "Puritanism."

Eliot did not avoid going "all the way to Rome" because he was prejudiced against Boston or St. Louis Catholics, but because the Church of England was the national church of his own origins with fully Catholic beliefs. Had he been an American of Swedish or German origins, now living in Stockholm or Berlin, he probably would have become a devout Lutheran. Eliot also approved of the connection between the religious, social, and political institutions which the Church of England enjoyed because it created social unity and moral order.

Once Gordon George's important Anglo-Catholic friends met Eliot, they began courting him because his "conversion" would be great publicity for the church. A few years earlier the Roman Catholic leadership in England had made a media event out of Chesterton's conversion.

Eliot was well aware of his dilemma. On the one hand he was an intensely private person and these decisions were his own. On the other hand, he had no intention of hiding his beliefs. But it was not his nature to proclaim them publicly in quite the way he liked to promulgate his literary judgments.

The result was that when Eliot made his decision to join the Church of England, he did not go to these highly visible leaders, but turned to William Stead, the American chaplain at Oxford. Eliot wrote to Stead to ask his help in being confirmed without any publicity because he hated "spectacular conversions." Stead responded by suggesting a plan that let only the few participants know. Then he asked whether or not Eliot had been baptized because his idea of Unitarians was an "austere people who abstain from baptism as well as communion." Stead explained that one must be baptized in the name of the Trinity before being confirmed, but that the baptism did not have to be an "Anglican" baptism.

Eliot wrote back to explain that his branch of Unitarians did practice baptism with water, as well as occasional communion services which his parents had attended regularly. He also asked if he must be ready to answer any questions or memorize the Confirmation Service in *The Book of Common Prayer*. Stead then explained that a Unitarian, not Trinitarian, baptism was not a true sacrament, so Eliot would need to be baptized as well as confirmed.

By May 1927 they had completed secret arrangements for Eliot to be baptized by Stead in the parish church at Finstock in the Cotswolds. Two Worcester professors would act as his sponsors (or godfathers). The next day Eliot would be confirmed at Oxford by the bishop in his private chapel. Those plans were carried out without fanfare on St. Peter's Day, June 29, 1927. Vivien Eliot did not come. Instead she began to complain that Tom had become a monk. Ezra Pound, too, heartily disliked his conversion.

Close friends of Eliot's like Herbert Read, I. A. Richards, Frank Morley, and Bonamy Dobrée became aware of his church membership because Eliot then began attending Early Church almost daily. But his conversion was not generally known until 1928, when he published a new literary manifesto called *For Lancelot Andrewes*.

Eliot's job provided him with firm, churchgoing friends in Geoffrey Faber and his wife Enid. Eliot soon began vacationing at their Welsh country home, and he confided in them more and more about his personal problems. Their son, Thomas Eliot Faber, was one of his godchildren, for whom Eliot wrote *Old Possum's Book of Practical Cats*.

The following November Eliot became a British subject. He did it, he told Virginia Woolf, because he was living and making a living in England. He liked his friends there, and he did not want to be a "squatter" who did not take full responsibility. Significantly, he did not mention his marriage as a reason.

In 1927 Faber & Faber published one of Eliot's best-known short poems, "Journey of the Magi," as an *Ariel* (Christmas) poem. Written in Eliot's Modernist, unadorned style, "Journey of the Magi" was based on a Christmas sermon of Bishop Andrewes. During their "long journey" there was clear Christian symbolism in the three trees seen against the low sky and the men dicing for silver at the inn. There was also a reference to the Communion Service phrase about Christ being "a perfect sacrifice, oblation and satisfaction for the sins of all men," and even an unexpected glimpse of Chesterton's old White Horse of Christendom.

The poem's modern diction probably served as a model for Dorothy L. Sayers when she began to write her realistic BBC religious dramas in the '30s. In *The Man Born to Be King*, Sayers's Wise Men also see Christ's end in his beginning. In the next few years Eliot wrote other *Ariel* poems for Faber & Faber: "A Song for Simeon," which used phrases from the "Nunc Dimittis," and "Animula," with its spiritual portrait of a childhood very like his own.

But the subtle message about Eliot's conversion did not get through to most of his readers. During the summer of 1928 Eliot's old Harvard professor, humanist philosopher Irving Babbitt, dined with Eliot on his way through London. Eliot felt he must tell Babbitt about his new religious beliefs and did so. According to Eliot, describing the episode in 1961, Babbitt then attacked him, not for "turning his coat," but for "not coming out in the open" with his public.

Certainly many modern converts to Christianity did not wear their religious hearts on their sleeves. It had been only because of a challenge issued to him in 1904 by a fellow journalist that G. K. Chesterton suddenly and publicly announced his commitment to Christian orthodoxy in the course of a newspaper debate with old Socialist Robert Blatchford. Eliot's contemporary, C. S. Lewis, after his reluctant conversion in 1929 (which he described as "the mouse's search for the cat") did not make the fact known outside his circle of friends until he began to write and broadcast Christian apologetics. Then, like many of Eliot's literary following, the

Oxford establishment became very disgruntled by Lewis's action.

But in 1928, nettled by Babbitt's accusation that he was being secretive, Eliot put one of his very "quotable sentences" into the preface of a book of essays. The result, as he admitted in 1961, was that those words "dogged" him long after they were a satisfactory statement of his social or literary opinions.

The famous sentence that confounded many of his literary admirers appeared in the preface of *For Lancelot Andrewes*. Just as his first "turning," *The Sacred Wood*, had been dedicated to his father, this second "turning" was dedicated to his mother. What few critics paid attention to was the frontispiece quotation from Bishop Andrewes, which Eliot adopted as his motto for doing battle as a crusader:

> Thou, Lord, Who walkest in the midst of the golden candlesticks, remove not, we pray Thee, our candlestick out of its place; but set in order the things which are wanting among us, and strengthen those which remain, and are ready to die.

In the preface Eliot said that he wanted to refute any accusation of "playing Possum" (Pound's old nickname for him). Then he stated that he was a "classicist in literature, a royalist in politics, and an Anglo-Catholic in religion." Those terms, used earlier by Charles Maurras, led a number of critics to assume that Eliot was also a Fascist. But, Eliot added, two of the three phrases were "claptrap," (i.e., slogans) and it was not his job to define the third. In the essays that followed, Eliot did carefully define what he meant by these terms, using the context of England, not France, and showing that his ideological similarity to Maurras was minimal.

In the first essay on Lancelot Andrewes, Eliot explored the unique cultural heritage of the Church of England as established under Elizabeth I. Then he described Andrewes's appeal for him. Andrewes was more medieval, bonded to the church and tradition, but much more a mystic than Donne. In his sermons Andrewes was wholly "in" his subject, so that he was "alone with the Alone." He was not a "personality" like Donne, who had sought refuge in religion from the "tumults of a strong emotional temperament."

Next, in a book review of a biography of Bishop Bramhall, Eliot described how the Bishop helped establish, then after Cromwell re-establish, the Church of England in Ireland. The Bishop had also debated with the philosopher Thomas Hobbes about church and state. Eliot said that Hobbes was a modern determinist whose world was that of Newton and Einstein. His true descendant was Bertrand Russell.

Bishop Bramhall had a sense of history so that his views on the relationship of church and state were a justification of the Anglican *via media*. Like Bishop Bramhall, Eliot considered the monarchy to be a unifying symbol, combining civic and religious responsibility.

As a Christian, Eliot himself remained remarkably ecumenical. He was impatient of sectarian controversy in a way reminiscent of C. S. Lewis. Eliot was an *incarnational* Christian, one for whom the coming of Christ was the most important event in history, which was reaffirmed by sacramental worship. But Eliot took a cool and observant stance about the behavior of the present-day Anglican Church. His published comments sound very like Dorothy L. Sayers when she declared that she was at her work of "bearding the bishops."

Then and now, however, a large number of Eliot's critics attacked him for turning "traitor" or "escapist" as well as "moralist." In *The Criterion*, for example, Eliot already was editorializing that "art for art's sake" was irrelevant because literature had a definite relationship to the social situation, a position soon taken by communists and fascists, too, in the doctrinaire '30s. But despite his effort to establish a middle ground for discourse and discussion in a extremist era, most of Eliot's statements were labeled a repudiation of Bloomsbury and the left, and a move to the right, or to fascism. Among the younger generation he had been a kind of god; now, he told Gordon George, to many in the intellectual community he had become not only a lost soul but a lost sheep.

Although American critics were not pleased with his political decision to be an Englishman, it was his Christian beliefs that were taken to be a real retreat from reality and democracy. Few understood what Eliot meant when he replied that orthodox Christianity did not soften the edges of life, but made them more cutting. At the same time, Eliot's public position did help to form a climate in which other Christian apologists could work.

In 1929 Eliot published his second appreciation of Dante, who continued to be his literary and spiritual master. He said that one could read

Dante without doing a great deal of scholarship because Dante wrote so lucidly, though his thought was not simple. Dante had a visual imagination and lived in an age when people still saw real visions, so he could make us see what he saw in clear images that reinforced one another. For any reader repelled by the end of *Inferno*, Eliot suggested he wait to judge Dante until he had read, and then lived for years, with the last canto of *Paradiso*.

Eliot felt that modern readers need not believe as Dante did but must understand Dante's world. Dante had given Eliot the sense of order and purpose which he had sought and found in the church. Eliot's ongoing Dantean discipleship helped to create Dante's impact on his generation as much as it suggested the structuring of Eliot's own poetry.

An interesting sidelight on his *Criterion* editorship was shown in a short, cordial correspondence between Eliot and Chesterton. Their brief exchange also points up the fact that both Chesterton and Eliot, as editors of small but important papers, read one another. Eliot first wrote on *Criterion* letterhead; later he used his own stationery, even scrawling notes by hand.

In a discussion of alliteration, Chesterton (typically) had misquoted Eliot from memory and wrote to apologize. Eliot wrote back to thank him and ask Chesterton to contribute some "unpopular statements" to *The Criterion*. Eliot added a "PS" saying Chesterton had assumed that most of his readers were "heretical ignorants."

In his next letter Eliot commented that, if quoted, he preferred to be quoted correctly. By the third letter Eliot was hoping to get Chesterton to write about humanism as a substitute for religion. By November 1928 Eliot was most politely trying to get a commitment from the chronically overextended GKC. It speaks well for their mutual admiration that Eliot did get Chesterton's contribution.

By May 1929 Eliot wrote to say how much he would like to visit Chesterton at Top Meadow when he spent a weekend with Herbert Read who lived in Beaconsfield. He added that he had great sympathy with Chesterton's political and social views and, "with obvious reservations," his religious views, and impulsively added that GKC's writing on Dickens "was always a delight."

In the last letters both men expressed dismay at their heavy schedules which kept them apart. A year later Eliot sent Chesterton a copy of Frank

Morrison's *Who Moved the Stone?*, an examination of the evidence about the Passion story by someone who began as a Modernist. It was a book Dorothy L. Sayers made great use of in *The Man Born to Be King*.

In a lighter vein, Eliot, like Sayers, wrote a number of detective story reviews in the late '20s. He had always been a Sherlock Holmes buff who could produce arcane details from the Holmes canon. He also approved of the "metaphysical" crime-and-punishment quality of detective fiction, in which he included Dostoyevsky's *Crime and Punishment*.

To his great sorrow, Eliot's mother died in 1929. His knowledge that by her standards he had not lived up to her hopes and ambitions for him intensified his loss. Instead he had joined a "reactionary " church, "retreated" from his American heritage, and wrote "modern" poetry. But whatever his sorrow—and Vivien Eliot said it was agonizing—Eliot commented later when heaped with honors that his mother would have been so pleased.

Ash-Wednesday, Eliot's next major poem, was published in 1930. In a 1959 talk at Chicago's Orchestra Hall Eliot said that after reading a portion of *The Waste Land*, he would next read part of *Ash-Wednesday* to give the audience some "relief." It may not have helped them. Although readers of this poem do not need to share Eliot's Christian faith, they do need to know the Christian Year, especially Lent, and the Ash Wednesday liturgy.

Structurally, Eliot built the poem on a phrase from Bishop Andrewes about the "two turnings" which Andrewes had declared were necessary for a "conversion." The one turning looked ahead to God; the other, appropriate for a penitential season, looked back to one's sinful past.

The style of Eliot's poem is simple and lucid, but its meaning is complicated and difficult. *Ash-Wednesday* combines intense personal emotions, often obscure to the reader, with the formal use of liturgical texts. It is the story of Eliot's conversion, both public and private—with all his skepticism and doubts still there, offered to God.

The stairs, a favorite Eliot metaphor, reflect Dante's staircase to heaven through Purgatory. They lead the poet to a third and final state, or turning, where he can glimpse a faith beyond hope and despair, where His peace is our will. Echoes of Dante's Paradise pervade the poem, as does the penitent's hope "to redeem the time."

PART THREE
Preacher 1930 – 1945

CHAPTER SEVEN

Anglican Retreat
1930 - 1934

*A*sh-Wednesday HAS BEEN DESCRIBED AS THE BEST EXAMPLE IN English literature of a poem that denies the world's images to see God directly. Because of its liturgical elements it has also been called a *Purgatorio*, reflecting the beginning of Eliot's climb up from *The Hollow Men*. But the poem seemed to show that Eliot was following the Negative Way by retreating from the world. Many critics therefore insisted that the poem was subjective and private. They described Eliot's Christianity as a peculiar, irregular version that lacked the central Christian tradition and showed elements of "romantic improvisation." That critical judgment turns Eliot's awareness of the difficulty of achieving spiritual balance into no more than a personal mannerism. Eliot's critics ignored the tradition of the Anglican Church, which had always acknowledged that it existed in a creative tension between Scripture and reason, tradition and experience. Eliot himself later wrote Helen Gardner that he considered *Ash-Wednesday* to be his Modernist version of Dante's *Vita Nuova*. He saw Dante's poem as an affirmation, since (as Charles Williams later described Dante's Beatrician vision) it first led Dante to a religious affirmation. Dante then harmonized his vision with the Catholic theological tradition.

After his confirmation Eliot had turned to Father Francis Underhill as his personal confessor. Father Underhill in turn had taken Eliot on retreat to Kelham Theological College near Nottingham. There Eliot met Brother George Every, who became a lifelong friend. Every also knew Charles Williams.

Brother George recalled that he first read *Ash-Wednesday* when he was struggling with his own vocation in a religious community. Every was learning painfully that a great gap existed between good desires and joy in love and service. Eliot's poem spoke to Every's condition because in it Eliot had enlarged the "dark night of the soul" by including every kind of modern difficulty, especially skepticism.

Every saw that in this approach Eliot was like Charles Williams. Both had confronted nothingness, so, in their ideal Christian society there would be some bright agnostics or skeptics who would continue the Anglican tradition of proportion by helping to preserve both Ways. Both Eliot and Williams, like G. K. Chesterton before them, saw ideological extremists and simplifiers as the true heretics.

As Eliot privately followed the routine of his new church, his public career continued to expand. Already as editor of *The Criterion* he had begun to speak out about political and social issues related to literature and its place in society. Now he began to be a Christian spokesman as well.

Eliot also remained a Modernist poet who sought new ways of translating Christianity into terms the contemporary world could understand. Every said that Eliot did not wish to write "Christmas-card gothic" and, in a letter to William Force Stead, Eliot said he was not writing devotional poetry but trying to describe the experience of searching for God.

Ash-Wednesday was well received, but when Eliot's conversion became publicly known, there was a general tendency to call him a reactionary who had reverted to an unprogressive and unscientific past. Eliot's belief in a classically structured society as a prerequisite for both order and liberty was seen as a snobbish insistence on class distinctions or even as a love of totalitarianism itself .

What Eliot was really preaching was the "civic virtue" that found meaning in history. It was his version of Charles Williams's "co-inherence" that was demanded by the City (or civilization) for the good of society. Instead of secular ideologies fighting one another, Eliot wanted to redevelop a balanced social and intellectual *via media* for Western civilization, using a spirit of rational cooperation and common sense.

Eliot was criticized by his followers from the Lost Generation, who had accepted the desolation of *The Waste Land* and believed in the Orphic arrogance of *The Sacred Wood*. Still others simply disliked his conversion and reacted spitefully. Young poet Stephen Spender, who had just met Eliot and found him the most approachable of the great writers, remembered Virginia Woolf's needling Eliot at teatime. She asked if he really went to church and if he passed the collection plate and how it felt to pray. Eliot answered Woolf politely and patiently.

Eliot's growing number of religious admirers, on the other hand, did not dismiss him as a C. S. Lewis "dinosaur." But they did tend to read a Christian meaning back into everything he had written, thus denying the reality of his conversion.

Eliot had originally dedicated *Ash-Wednesday* to Vivien, but his religion was both incomprehensible and threatening to her. The Eliots now lived near St. Cyprian's Church, where Eliot went daily after he was confirmed. He and Vivien were almost living apart. He was at work all day, met friends or literary contacts at lunch, and went to literary gatherings. He did his *Criterion* editing and his own writing at night or on weekends.

Vivien's health had greatly deteriorated, partly from stress and illnesses, partly from the effects of treatments she was given. It seems likely that her condition began with a hormonal imbalance which could be dealt with easily today. At the time, although Vivien had the best medical advice available, it did her little good.

In and out of nursing homes, she rarely accompanied Eliot anywhere. She was not asked back to the Woolfs because she upset Virginia. She had begun to resent Eliot's fame, and her discontent led her to cause outrageous scenes that upset her husband and embarrassed and alienated his friends. To Eliot's friends it seemed she had become not just hostile but irrational.

From what is known about the Eliot marriage, it seems that Vivien had been a charming and talented young woman with whom Eliot fell madly in love. He loved her for the very qualities of spontaneous gaiety and unpredictable moods he later found it impossible to live with. Vivien perhaps fell in love with the idea of marrying a poet and being his partner in a great literary career. How much she cared about her own career is not clear. But neither of them could have foreseen that her increasingly serious physical and mental problems, and Eliot's low physical vitality and disciplined ambition, would mean that they could not achieve a workable marriage.

By the early 1930s Eliot's family, friends, and religious adviser were all telling him that he must leave Vivien. Their separation would probably not be a good solution for her, although the past ten years had demonstrated that living with Eliot did not do her much good either. Her brother Maurice long afterward blamed Eliot for "not being kind to Vivie," but it was a role neither he nor her mother offered to undertake.

If Eliot had done something wilder, more romantic, like taking off with another woman as his friend Pound did, his critics might have excused his behavior. What they still cannot understand was his matter-of-fact acceptance of responsibility for the decision, or his resultant lifestyle. Any suggestion that Eliot had no abiding sense of guilt about Vivien and his retreat from the marriage is made ridiculous by considering his later work, principally *The Family Reunion* and *The Cocktail Party*.

When Eliot finally bowed to the judgment of his confessor that he must separate from Vivien—and without the church he might never have been able to make the decision—he knew he could neither divorce Vivien nor remarry until she died. That was the official position of the Church of England, but the fact that he took the church's teaching seriously is seen by some critics as a sign of psychological disturbance. It is still used to suggest that Eliot was too timid to live dangerously or that he then took advantage of other women with whom he was friends because he refused to become intimate with them.

While Eliot tried to get up his nerve to make the break with Vivien, George Bell, Dean of Canterbury Cathedral, became Bishop of

Chichester. Bishop Bell had participated in the recent effort to reform the Prayer Book to allow more Anglo-Catholic practices. Bell was also a leader in the worldwide ecumenical movement, and was a friend of German theologian Dietrich Bonhoeffer.

The new bishop was determined to involve the church in the arts, in order to make use of all the trump cards it held. The result was that he became a friend not only of Eliot's, but of Charles Williams and Dorothy L. Sayers. In 1925, with the help of Margaret Babington, Bell had founded the Friends of Canterbury Cathedral. This energetic group began the Canterbury Festival which sponsored cathedral productions of Christian plays. They used the proceeds to pay for cathedral repairs.

Recognizing that Eliot was an ace of trumps, Bishop Bell invited the Eliots to Chichester for a weekend, together with his new Director of Religious Drama, actor-producer E. Martin Browne. When Vivien refused to go, Eliot went alone; Browne said later that he was very silent.

At the bishop's request, Eliot read *Ash-Wednesday* to the guests, but refused to explain any of its lines. This rather unsuccessful weekend, however, was to result in Eliot's not only becoming a successful playwright, but in his making two firm friends in Bishop Bell and Martin Browne.

Eliot was still working hard at his other jobs. As an editor at Faber & Faber he almost singlehandedly shaped English poetry from the '30s to the '60s, in what is generally known as the "Age of Eliot." He published W. H. Auden and other younger poets like Louis MacNeice, C. Day Lewis, and Stephen Spender; the late Poet Laureate, Sir John Betjeman; and still later, Ted Hughes, the present Poet Laureate of England. Hughes is the former husband of American poet Sylvia Plath. There was a Plath-like quality about Vivien Eliot, but because of Eliot's reticence, it is likely that the two men never discussed it.

Unlike many of his contemporaries, Eliot could appreciate work he disagreed with in both poetry and prose. At *The Criterion* he tried hard to publish a wide range of opinion. In particular, he treated communist writers as representatives of another religious viewpoint, which must be taken seriously.

At Faber & Faber he was still publishing James Joyce and Ezra Pound. Pound had completely alienated Harriet Monroe of *Poetry*, who wrote to Eliot to complain that Pound was calling her names and insisting she had to publish cantos that were nothing but his own political and economic views. Eliot wrote her back a soothing letter, saying that Pound wrote abusively to everybody. He admitted he too knew less and less about what Pound was saying, but continued to admire his technical skill.

As was typical of him in times of great personal stress, Eliot was unable to complete another major poem between *Ash-Wednesday* in 1930 and his pageant play, *The Rock*, which was performed in 1934. But he began another poem, and two fragments were later published with "Sweeney Agonistes" as *Unfinished Poems*. These poems were called "Coriolan," after Shakespeare's upright Roman general who was first made much of, but who was then destroyed by his own city and family.

The first poem was "Triumphal March"; the second, "Difficulties of a Statesman." In them the poet adopted the persona of an Isaiah-like prophet, seeking to show the interconnection between past and contemporary history and to comment ironically on the present scene.

At this point in the '30s, the Great Depression had started; the Japanese had conquered Manchuria; Mussolini had made Italian trains run on time and was looking at Ethiopia; and the Nazis had won over one hundred seats in the German Reichstag. Labourite guru G. B. Shaw was visiting and admiring Russia's Josef Stalin; Spain had become an uneasy republic; England, with three million unemployed, had turned to the Baldwin Conservatives and gone off the Gold Standard.

The Coriolan poems resembled Eliot's *Criterion* editorials. In them, like Chesterton in *G. K.'s Weekly*, Eliot called for governments that were less international and more responsive than coalition governments by committee, made up of old gangs of politicians. He also deplored world-wide overindustrialization and unemployment. For Eliot and Chesterton, capitalism and socialism were Tweedledum and Tweedledee, whose combat would not bring in the Millennium. Eliot's Coriolan sought a return by the City itself to religious and moral principles for everyone.

In 1931 Eliot wrote a strong criticism of the recent Lambeth Conference. He began "Thoughts After Lambeth" by saying that the Church of England might wash its dirty linen in public, but at least it did wash it. Conferences like Lambeth were not meant to produce papal encyclicals, which demanded definite actions, but to show where the church was heading, so Eliot excused the three hundred bishops for producing "woolly thinking."

As Chesterton had done in *Heretics*, Eliot then explained that he had been won over to Christianity by the arguments of great heretics like Bertrand Russell. Eliot took it as a hopeful sign that being a Christian was no longer respectable. He felt that, to appeal to the young, a religion must make demands on its believers rather than preach Russell's gospel of happiness.

He noted that the Church of England had just lost a twenty-year battle for Prayer Book reform because of the evangelical cry "No Popery." Observers were convinced that the Anglo-Catholics might leave the church, as the Methodists had done, and that it was essential that the church be disestablished to prevent that. But Eliot disagreed. He said he was one of those "revolutionary" Anglo-Catholics who liked both the Elizabethan church-state relationship and the Anglo-Catholic emphasis on worship and liturgy.

While the Church of England allowed all "allowable exceptions," the Church of Rome had only principles, which meant it had to deal with the exceptions. As a result, Eliot felt that the Church of England had both the best chance to reunite Christendom and a duty to work to that end in a world that was developing a non-Christian culture and bias.

In 1932 the chance came for Eliot to leave Vivien for good, without a drawn-out confrontation, which he felt too weak to carry through. Harvard University asked him to spend the 1932-33 academic year in America as the Charles Eliot Norton Professor, an honor that would have greatly pleased his mother. Since he had to give only eight lectures from November to March, he could make up for his lost salary at Faber & Faber with other lectures. Eliot spent the spring preparing material for *The Criterion* while he was gone. He also gave the first of what were to be many talks on the BBC, speaking about "The Modern Dilemma" of being a Christian.

Nothing was said about a permanent separation to Vivien, who was very upset at his departure. Her mother and brother agreed with Eliot's other advisers that their separation was inevitable; the main problem was how to care for Vivien. In September, after Vivien gave a farewell party for him, her brother and his wife drove the couple to Southampton, where Eliot boarded his ship. By the time he arrived in

America, his *Selected Essays*, containing most of his prose since 1917, had been published there and in England.

In the United States some treated Eliot as a literary VIP and a returning native son. But he was also disliked for his "phony" Englishness and resented for his position as a literary authority. Robert Frost, for example, found him "condescending."

Eliot lived near the Harvard campus and held weekly, very English tea parties for his students. He also saw a great deal of his family, some of whom, like his cousin Eleanor Hinkley, lived in Cambridge. But he was homesick for England and still felt "stifled" by academic Harvard and the "Eastern Establishment."

In America, Franklin D. Roosevelt was elected President and the New Deal began. Eliot kept up with American politics and issues, which, unlike the typical Englishman, he also understood. But Eliot was not a New Dealer, and much later he admitted to William Turner Levy that he blamed Roosevelt for playing with the safety of England during the war.

Eliot had little time before leaving England to prepare lectures, so he had chosen to speak about something he knew well. This was the history of English literary criticism, especially the poet-critics like Dryden, Coleridge, and Matthew Arnold. His lectures were published the following November 1933 under the title *The Use of Poetry and the Use of Criticism*.

This lecture series had to be published by the terms of his contract, but whenever possible, Eliot not only gave talks but created books out of his lectures to augment his income. Other writers all did the same thing. Sayers and Lewis refused to go on the lucrative American lecture circuit, but Chesterton came twice during the 1930s, and Eliot, like Auden, was to do it, except for the war years, for the rest of his life. From now on these writers also spoke regularly on the BBC. Eliot admitted that he preferred writing to speaking and was always nervous beforehand. He also preferred to read a lecture to reading his own work, an experience he found exhausting.

In his Harvard lectures Eliot hoped to develop a new poetics that took into account his religious beliefs. He felt he had a right to change his position from the one he took in *The Sacred Wood*, but Eliot critics tend to ignore the chronology of his life or thought. Years later in the

1964 edition of *The Use of Poetry and the Use of Criticism*, Eliot remarked he still hoped that people would quit republishing "Tradition and the Individual Talent." Then a student might be able to pass an examination on him, without using the phrases "dissociation of sensibility" or "objective correlative."

In his opening lecture Eliot paid tribute to Harvard's Charles Eliot Norton, a good and moral Stoic, who had lived in a decaying, non-Christian world but still assumed that literature had permanent importance because the poetry of a people represents its highest consciousness. Eliot then explored the relationship between poetry and criticism. Criticism looked at poetry's uses or judged actual poems. A critic's aesthetic and moral position must be consistent, but it need not agree with Eliot's views. Criticism was especially important when a poet could not communicate with a whole people; his difficulty was even greater when he was speaking to a clique or only to himself.

Eliot thought that the big change in poetry came at the end of the eighteenth century, when poets like Wordsworth and Coleridge became its "priests." Then, by the nineteenth century, Matthew Arnold had made poetry a substitute for religion. Today Eliot felt that psychology led critics to "fantastic excesses" in trying to discover the mind of the poet and the mind of the reader. Sociology, on the other hand, led to the study of poetry in relation to its own time and place. As a result there was no general agreement on what poetry is or does.

Eliot suggested that a poem's existence was really located somewhere between the writer and reader. Its reality lay not only in what the writer said or in his or her experience writing it, but also in the reader's experience. Eliot hoped that his poetry would be enjoyed by as large and various a group of people as possible, but he was not convinced that teaching poetry appreciation was a good idea. In his discussion Eliot foreshadowed much of Dorothy L. Sayers's chapter on the "Problem Picture" in *The Mind of the Maker*.

As an example of what he meant, Eliot compared Jacques Maritain and I. A. Richards. The "pagan" Richards had announced that Eliot's poetry showed that sex was the problem of this generation, just as religion had been for the older one. Eliot said that things like sex and religion are not problems like "Free Trade" or "Imperial Preference"; the human race had existed for centuries without considering them problems at all.

On the other hand, Jacques Maritain was a Thomist theologian who wanted to establish poetry's position in a Christian world. Eliot agreed with Maritain that religion kept poetry from believing itself destined to reform life, but Eliot still wanted more of a *via media* for poetry than Maritain.

As he saw it, a poet may be driven to write a poem but by the time the poem is written, the original experience is unrecognizable, and the poem communicates something that did not exist before. In addition, every age wants different things from poetry, but new poets can also change what the age wants, so that no one time can "embrace or exhaust all the uses of poetry." For a poet today who wanted to have some direct "social utility" and reach a larger audience, the theater would be the best place to work. But, as things were, poetry was not a career but "a mug's game."

During his year in America Eliot took a number of trips to give lectures. He toured California, went to St. Louis, New York, and Buffalo; spoke at Johns Hopkins, Yale, and Princeton. Eliot also spoke at Bryn Mawr and Mount Holyoke, and saw a production of "Sweeney Agonistes" put on by Vassar students.

In the middle of his busy life, in February 1933 Eliot wrote his London solicitor and asked him to prepare a legal Deed of Separation. He enclosed a letter to be personally delivered to Vivien by the lawyer. He later told a friend that the act of mailing that letter had made him think of the lines in *Julius Caesar*:

> Between the acting of a dreadful thing
> And the first motion, all the interim is
> Like a phantasma, or a hideous dream.

Eliot had arranged for Vivien to keep their apartment, and she continued to live there until her breakdown just as World War II began. Except by accident, Eliot saw her again only in their solicitor's office; he felt he could not handle a private meeting. Vivien continued to hope or plot for him to "come home." She went places where he might be, or did silly, sad things like pushing chocolate candy bars through the Faber &

Faber mail slot, hoping to get into his office—forcing his friends and colleagues to meet her, or help him escape out the back way.

In April 1933 Eliot went south to the University of Virginia, where he gave the Page-Barbour Lectures. Like the Norton lectures at Harvard, it was part of the arrangement that his lectures be published, and they appeared in 1933 with the title *After Strange Gods: A Primer of Modern Heresy*.

In these talks Eliot was continuing his effort to stand literary criticism on its head by changing the critical debate to allow moral judgments. He was beginning to define what he meant by the Christian City, or society, and to develop appropriate social concerns. But some of his remarks gave him an uncalled-for reputation as a bigoted Wasp and anti-Semite, and Eliot never allowed the book to be reprinted.

Although Eliot told the audience that he was speaking as a "moralist," not as a critic, his literary stature worked against him. Many commentators objected to his attempt to reintroduce ethics into aesthetics, just as Eliot objected to their determination to turn literature into a religion. Essentially, the argument with the book came from intellectuals who felt that Eliot had taken up an anti-intellectual stance by daring to judge the great modern writers, especially his own friends, by Christian standards.

In spite of those objections, this small book led toward his later social commentary. It is Eliot's version of Chesterton's *Heretics*, *Orthodoxy*, and *The Everlasting Man*, and Eliot even used Chesterton's terms "orthodox" and "heretic" instead of his earlier critical terms "classical" and "romantic." Many of his basic ideas were to reappear in Dorothy L. Sayers's 1944 Edward Alleyn Lecture called "Towards a Christian Aesthetic." C. S. Lewis's position on literary criticism was very similar as well.

What *After Strange Gods* lacks is the genial Chestertonian use of absurdity to pin his opponents to the mat. The tone of Eliot's talks was serious, but not "savage and contemptuous," if you agree with Eliot's assumption that Christian orthodoxy was an appropriate viewpoint for considering literature. And, as Eliot explained in his preface, in using modern writers whose work he knew well, he was not necessarily accusing these artists of blasphemy, but was trying to show how he had come to see that literary problems are not merely literary.

Eliot was also specifically encouraging Southern listeners to appreciate their own, still homogeneous regional culture, which he believed provided them with a fertile ground for creativity. Compared to the rest of America in the mid-twentieth century, Eliot saw that the South still had a definite tradition. As a New Englander, Eliot said he had found that crossing the Potomac River was like crossing from England into Wales.

A Southern literary flowering, however, would not occur because the South had dogmatic beliefs, but because it had the habits and customs of the same people living in the same place. At the same time Eliot insisted that traditions should not be kept for sentimental reasons or to maintain superiority over others. Tradition was always both good and bad and must be carefully reexamined (or repossessed) by every generation. To be productive a culture also needed to have a "unity of religious beliefs." This meant that too many aliens, or "freethinking Jews," was undesirable.

That one phrase has been used to condemn Eliot as anti-Semitic, but that designation derives largely from our heightened post-Holocaust sensitivities. What Eliot was trying to say was that great cosmopolitan cultures like Rome produced cosmopolitan works, which destroyed the moral instincts of the native population and ultimately the civilization itself. It is regrettable that in the tight little island of England, despite its imperial orbit, "Jew" was a quickly understood symbol for "alien." This point was well made by George Orwell, who wrote that the charge against Eliot was totally false. Before the war "everyone had used offensive terms" much the way postwar writers now sneered at "Anglo-Indian colonels in boarding houses."

Eliot's underlying assumption is valid because, as his poem *The Waste Land* had demonstrated, a community divided against itself is not a City with common assumptions that can give the artist a basis for communication. What Eliot was "preaching" was that there is little truth in the popular idea that a multi-racial, multi-ethnic, multi-religious community which practices only a "civil religion" will nurture great works of art. He himself had been made a Christian writer by his conscious return to his more homogeneous past.

Eliot used the term "tradition" with the term "orthodoxy," making both terms opposites for "heterodoxy" or "heresy." By tradition Eliot meant an almost unconscious way of feeling and acting which had been common to a society over a long period of time. Orthodoxy, on the other hand, required thought and could be defended by a single individual. Orthodoxy implied classical Christian beliefs, as well as the opposite of the heresy of glorifying novelty or originality for their own sake.

Eliot also recognized that tradition never stayed still and everyone had some heretical viewpoints because all "heresies" were partly right. But as Chesterton had pointed out in *Heretics*, modern heretics' philosophies were "quite solid, quite coherent and quite wrong." Eliot added that heresies had a "seductive simplicity" that was more believable than the truth.

In relating these ideas to his own writing, Eliot explained that in his experience the breakdown of tradition meant that every artist was on his own. As a result it was all too easy for a writer to decide he was the chosen leader of a new movement and play the role of a messiah.

Eliot then described a number of his contemporaries whom he felt had done so, citing as examples Katherine Mansfield, James Joyce, D. H. Lawrence, Irving Babbitt, Ezra Pound, and W. B. Yeats. By rejecting Christianity, they all had grown up outside a living tradition. Pound, for example, admired everything about the Middle Ages except what made them significant: their beliefs. That was reminiscent of Chesterton's comment that John Ruskin admired everything about a gothic church except the altar.

Also like Chesterton, Eliot said that blasphemy was now only "bad form without any belief," and, in a world where real blasphemy was impossible, an artist had to create his view of life by exploiting his own personality. Beyond this "personalized" heresy, Eliot had found that the diabolical operated in the modern world through men of excellent character, for whom original sin was not real. It taught him that tradition must be continually "criticized" by orthodoxy, because, when there were no objective standards to judge an artist's work, literary taste was formed by the power of one "seductive" personality after another. In saying this, Eliot was certainly accusing himself, too, as the creator of *The Waste Land*.

In June 1934 Eliot finally returned to England. Just before he sailed, he had spoken to the graduates of Milton Academy in a speech that seemed to be addressed to himself. Among other things, Eliot told the

Milton students that at some time they would have to make "an ir-
revocable choice" and then face the consequences. Despite his marital
situation, Eliot had a good time in America. He enjoyed seeing a New
England fall again, visiting with his family, and renewing his friendship
with Bostonian Emily Hale.

He planned to keep out of Vivien's way until she accepted their
separation as final. But she became distraught, and friends and relatives
had to keep an eye on her as she began to engage in more and more
bizarre behavior. Eliot stayed only a few days in London, then went to
Surrey where he rented a room near the home of Frank Morley at Pikes
Farm. The Morley family, who were to be given the Eliot "Donkey
Book," were unconventional in a Chestertonian, Distributist way.
They made their own clothes and baked their own bread.

Every Sunday Eliot walked down the country lane a mile to St.
George's Church, Crowhurst, for Early Communion. Eliot spoke that
summer to the Anglo-Catholic Summer School of Sociology at Keble
College, Oxford, home of the Oxford Movement. He spoke on
"Catholicism and International Order," and said that he had no objec-
tion in this confused age to being called a bigot for having absolute
ideals in political and social behavior. In August he went to visit the
Faber family in Wales; in September he stayed at the Anglican
Theological College at Kelham.

The fall of 1934 Gordon George found Eliot a place to live in London at 33 Courtfield Road in Kensington. It was a boarding house run
by an eccentric individual named William Scott-Hall, a former Roman
Catholic whose career included ordination as a bishop in the Old
Catholic Church and a stint as an officer in the British Army. Miss
Frieda Bevan really ran the household, and Eliot was very fond of her
cat Bubbles. St. Stephen's Church, Gloucester Road, was nearby, and
its vicar, Father Eric Cheetham, now became a close friend.

CHAPTER EIGHT

Difficulties of a Statesman 1934 - 1939

*E*LIOT NOW BEGAN TO LIVE AN AUSTERE PRIVATE LIFE, CHARACTERIZED by personal discipline and by responsibilities in the church. Not long after he returned to London, Father Eric Cheetham asked him to become the vicar's (or senior) warden, the highest lay position in the parish. Eliot accepted the job, and kept it until 1959. He had to administer parish finances and take up the collection. He also regularly attended weekday Mass (or Early Church), worshipping in St. Stephen's green and gold Edwardian splendor for more than forty years.

As an Anglo-Catholic parish, St. Stephen's sevices were "high," that is, very formal, often chanted instead of spoken. The minister was called Father Cheetham, and there was careful observance of fast and feast days. The Eucharist was celebrated daily and at both services on Sundays, and Anglo-Catholics always fasted before taking communion. A lighted red lamp hung in the chancel to indicate that the Sacrament (consecrated elements of the Lord's Supper) was always kept there. The church kept a faint smell of the incense used on holy days and had narrow pews that made kneeling uncomfortable. The Anglo-Catholic wing of the Anglican Church was to gain great strength and authority during the next three decades, finally imposing many of its practices on the Anglican Church worldwide.

Soon after Eliot became vicar's warden, Father Cheetham invited him to come live in the parish house of St. Stephen's at 9 Grenville Place. Eliot accepted and stayed there for the next five years. He did not live with or share meals with the parish clergy, but only rented inexpensive rooms there, which allowed him to live an almost cloistered life. He kept the address a secret from many of his friends, so that his wife could not track him down. When Virginia Woolf visited him, she was depressed by his dark green rooms with their odd pieces of furniture and broken-down bookcases.

Eliot also joined the St. Stephen's clergy on a retreat held at St. Simon's, Kentish Town, where he met two other clergymen who made a great difference to his personal religious life. They were Father Philip Bacon and Father Frank Hillier. Hillier was Eliot's age; Bacon, older, and an invalid. After they met, Eliot arranged to have Father Bacon become his confessor. He then drove to Kentish Town every few months where he made his confession and then joined both men at lunch. When Father Bacon became too ill, Eliot turned to Father Hillier.

Both going to confession and regular attendance at church helped to sustain Eliot in the habit of belief. It was not a playwright's appreciation of the "drama" of High Church rituals that gradually convinced Eliot that his chronic melancholy could be lifted, or his sense of guilt removed, but his daily life of holy routine.

Eliot's sister Marian came to visit him in 1934 when his old Boston acquaintance Emily Hale also made the first of a series of summer trips to England. But Eliot's social life centered about his friends at Faber & Faber and contributors to *The Criterion*. At work, American Frank Morley used to help "English" Eliot pull off elaborate pranks with firecrackers to celebrate the Fourth of July. Geoffrey Faber and Frank Morley both went with Eliot to parties given by John Hayward, whom Eliot had met at Cambridge in 1926 when Hayward was one of six bright undergraduates chosen to breakfast with him.

Hayward, who had muscular dystrophy and was progressively

disabled, had gone to King's College, Cambridge, before coming to London. He became a professional man of letters, compiling anthologies, editing editions of the classics, and contributing to journals like *The Criterion*. Later Hayward not only edited Penguin's 1953 *T. S. Eliot: Selected Prose*, but also collected working drafts of Eliot's plays which he gave to his college. Hayward was famous for holding lively, amusing parties at his home at 22 Bina Gardens, near Eliot's own rooms. Eliot's fondness for clever verses and practical jokes was put to good use, and some of their partying ended up in a privately published collection called *Noctes Binanianae*.

Before moving to 9 Grenville Place, Eliot had begun work in 1933 on an entirely new project which confounded old friends like the Woolfs. It was a pageant play called *The Rock*, which represented a watershed in his writing career. It was not only directed toward a different audience, but it also established Eliot publicly as a Chestertonian "Defendent" of the Church of England.

Eliot had already shown that he was intrigued by poetic drama, both as a way of communicating with a larger audience and of overcoming the "difficulty" of his poetry. (Even Virginia Woolf had plaintively complained she had to make dizzy and dangerous leaps from one line to the next and longed for "the old decorums.") But Eliot had found little scope for such experiments outside the small art theaters. His dramatic fragment, "Sweeney Agonistes," was put on in 1934 by Rupert Doone at the experimental Group Theatre, where poetic dramas by younger poets like Auden and Isherwood, Spender and MacNeice, were being performed.

Oxford don Nevill Coghill, the Inkling who had helped C. S. Lewis with his "anti-Eliot" poetry campaign, had found that his prize student, W. H. Auden, like Lewis's student John Betjeman, admired Eliot's work. Coghill tried reading Eliot, but it was not until he read "Sweeney Agonistes" that he was conquered. Coghill went to see the Doone production, which took place before an audience of thirty people, but Doone interpreted the play as a study in a murderer's psychology, not as the soul's need to lose the love of created beings. When he met Eliot at Oxford's All Souls College, Coghill asked if he had been astonished at that interpretation of the play. Eliot admitted he had been, but the play obviously

could have different meanings and the author's view was not necessarily "right."

Vivien Eliot found "Sweeney Agonistes," who tries to murder his
way out of his dilemma with his girlfriend Doris, unpleasantly
biographical. She came to a performance and sat in the front row. She
also turned up at an Eliot book signing for his *Collected Poems*, bringing their dog Polly. This was the last time they ever met.

In the meantime, Martin Browne had asked Eliot to write the
words for a pageant to raise funds to build suburban churches for
the Diocese of London. It was just ten years since Eliot had
marched with his friends the Dobrées in a London demonstration,
singing "Onward Christian Soldiers," to protest a plan to destroy a
number of the old City churches.

Apart from the avant-garde theater, by the late nineteenth century
there had been successful productions of verse dramas like Tennyson's
Becket, Shelley's *Cenci*, and Gilbert Murray's translations of Euripides.
The public attitude, based on the Puritan tradition that had banned
plays from church precincts, was being changed by the Anglo-Catholic
emphasis on the church's medieval tradition, while the English fondness
for oratorios like Handel's *Messiah* and Mendelssohn's *Elijah* had
created large amateur choruses.

The pageant was another English institution, made up of a series of
tableaux, rather like a stationary parade. Eliot's pageant was to be put
on at Sadler's Wells Theatre. Like the Old Vic, that theater was run by
a remarkable woman, Lilian Baylis, a practicing Christian as well as a
great theatrical character.

The London committee wanted each parish to do a scene from
London's history. Browne wanted to focus on the present, but had
trouble convincing the committee that T. S. Eliot was the right man.
"Too modern, too difficult," they said. Browne countered that Eliot was
the major poet of the time, one who wrote with a Modernist voice
which was also the voice of a prophet who had ended his pilgrimage of
faith in the church. Browne won.

Some critics regarded Eliot's continuing "obsession" with poetic
drama as "religiosity" and "bourgeois humbug." For them sin was not
worse than crime; it was simply less effective drama. Beginning with *The
Rock*, however, Eliot's plays won him increasing public acclaim and

recognition. They were also his most public commentary on the human condition, in which he emphasized the Christian understanding of a "call" or "vocation." Taken as a whole Eliot's plays have been described as "one of the major efforts of the modern literary imagination."

Eliot's first two plays represent a distinct group of overtly religious verse drama. *The Rock*, produced in 1934, was the immediate predecessor of *Murder in the Cathedral*. Eliot had agreed to write the necessary words for one hundred pounds. He and Browne met for lunch about once a month at the Garrick Club to develop the structure and choose the scenes. Despite Browne's protests, Eliot refused to be called the author of the play, and he reprinted only the choral passages in collections of his poetry.

The onstage action of *The Rock* is the building of a church. That process was intended to symbolize the endless building and rebuilding of the church throughout history. The modern Cockney workmen speak for mankind, but they are also able to speak with people from London's past, from the Danes to Sir Christopher Wren. Together the choruses and actors represent the church as both a physical community in a real place and as the "communion of saints" in time.

Eliot's ten stylized choruses, despite their stiffness, show he was learning how to use a chorus for dramatic exposition. The verse is powerful, measured, and meticulous, but sounds too much like Eliot the preacher, without the fluidity needed for a group. Eliot had written to Paul Elmer More that he was writing under the inspiration of Isaiah and Ezekiel, as he had done in his Coriolan poems. The major character in the choruses is the Rock, who represented the church itself, not St. Peter.

Eliot also engaged in contemporary social criticism, using stylized characters reminiscent of those in Sayers's early verse play, "The Mocking of Christ." In one scene he satirized communism and fascism, using choreographed groups of Red Shirts and Black Shirts. Then he brought on a suave Plutocrat, who said he stood for church, state, and liberty, but produced a golden calf called power. Eliot also dramatized a strong plea for work for the unemployed, while defending man's need for churches as much as for housing.

While working on *The Rock* Eliot saw himself as a craftsman learning his trade; he was a shy and silent witness of rehearsals. Although he

sent gifts to acknowledge his leading ladies and showed great appreciation and support for Browne, Browne's wife, and the others involved,
Eliot remained an observer in the shadows.

Getting thirty parishes of amateur actors to work together, as
well as costumes, sets, and music, was a formidable job, and Eliot
was visibly depressed at the last rehearsals. But the pageant
worked. It had nightly audiences of 1,500 or more and was both a
critical and popular success.

Bishop Bell of Chichester came to see *The Rock* and, pleased with
the play and its reception by the public, then asked Eliot to write the
first original play commissioned for the Canterbury Festival. To pay
Eliot, the bishop could offer only one hundred pounds made from previous productions.

Eliot accepted the commission and chose to write about the
cathedral's "own" saint, Thomas á Becket, although there were already
a number of other plays about him. During the Middle Ages, Thomas
á Becket had been the most popular saint in Western Europe, and the
cathedral had become his shrine. Eliot not only shared his very name,
but he felt he had a personal understanding of Becket's temptation "to
do the right thing for the wrong reason."

As always, making use of traditional sources, Eliot studied the earlier plays on Becket and the historical records. His play, however, did
not focus exclusively on the psychological and spiritual aspect of
Becket's martyrdom, but like *The Rock* also derived its importance
from the social conflict between church and state. Like his Becket, Eliot
believed that society should be run by the law of God, to provide
human beings with outward order and inner peace. The church had appeared to lose with Becket's death, but in fact it had won. Eliot used the
chorus of women of Canterbury to involve the ordinary people in what
had happened to their archbishop. He made them come alive, first to
their own share of the guilt, and then to a realization of the redemptive
power of Christ's death, shown forth by the martyrdom.

Eliot was acutely aware of the fact that his play was to be performed—like Greek tragedy celebrating a cultic event—near the site of
the murder of Becket, which took place at the foot of the northern steps
from the nave that lead to the cloisters and the chapter house. At the
murder site today is a modern triple cross and altar, before which Pope

John Paul II and the Archbishop of Canterbury knelt together in 1983. In the undercroft of the cathedral at the altar to twentieth-century martyrs, there is also a line from Eliot's play: ". . . the blood of Thy martyrs and saints/Shall enrich the earth."

Eliot aimed at writing a "neutral" verse like the kind used in *Everyman*, but he also made Modernist use of an abrupt transition to modern dialogue like G. B. Shaw's last scene in *Saint Joan* when Eliot's four tempters (or murderers) defend themselves to the audience, subtly echoing Becket's own temptations. His 1935 audiences equated their self-serving remarks with the statements made by the Nazis who had recently come to power in Germany. Eliot's chorus, derived from Greek tragedy, was also made up of women and contained liturgical elements of choir, congregation (or audience) and priests. Becket's prose sermon on Christmas morning was based in part on historical records, but it was also another Eliot version of Bishop Lancelot Andrewes's sermon on the Nativity.

Ultimately, Eliot's play is neither a biography of Becket nor a slice of social history. He used the theme central to all his subsequent plays: the role of the saints, or the elect, in renewing the body of Christ. Its dramatic development comes first from Becket's own growth in understanding that a true martyr no longer desires anything for himself, even the glory of martyrdom. Then his understanding is made contemporary and personal for the audience/congregation through the chorus. Becket's martydom will not redeem the land unless it is accepted by the people and church for whom he was murdered.

Eliot stipulated that Martin Browne must produce the play. Browne was to produce all of Eliot's plays, an example of Eliot's preference for working with friends and his intense loyalty to them. Its thriller title was suggested by Browne's actress wife. The play was performed at Canterbury on a small open stage at one end of the rectangular Chapter House. There are wooden monks' stalls around the high, windowless stone walls, and only one entrance up the center aisle.

These Canterbury productions, under the energetic leadership of Margaret Babington, were community affairs, with local businesses, schools, and cathedral personnel all taking part. Most of the actors were amateurs. A young Roman Catholic actor named Robert Speaight was asked to play Becket just as he set out for Rome to participate in the canonization of the English saints John Fisher and Sir Thomas More. The part of Becket not only made Speaight's name in the theater, but it led to his playing the part of Jesus Christ in Dorothy L. Sayers's BBC cycle, *The Man Born to Be King*.

At Canterbury, the play ran only an hour and a half with no break. The chorus of women had to stay onstage throughout. At Durham Cathedral in 1983 it was effectively performed at dusk in the Galilee Chapel, where the sound of chorus and knights, rushing in and out among the pillars, disturbed the eternal rest of the Venerable Bede, buried beside the altar beneath a black onyx slab. *Murder in the Cathedral*, still Eliot's most popular play, has been performed many times in many places, but Eliot and others like Robert Speaight felt that it is best suited to a church setting.

Murder in the Cathedral was produced at Canterbury on June 15, 1935, and was acclaimed the next day as "a turning point in English drama." It opened again on All Saints' Day 1935 at the Mercury Theatre in London. There it startled Eliot by having a successful West End run, even surviving the crisis of church and state brought on by the abdication of Edward VIII.

By now Eliot's literary peers had a clear idea of what his conversion was going to mean to his writing and editing, and many disapproved. Some considered his growing social acceptance with church leaders and society a sign of selling out. The King and Queen, for example, had come to see a performance and Eliot had sat with them. G. K. Chesterton's wife Frances also came to the Mercury Theatre to try out its seats, but they were too narrow to hold the huge GKC. This fact saddened Robert Speaight, who was convinced that the play might have been written just for Chesterton.

While he worked as a religious playwright, Eliot continued to function as an editor at Faber & Faber. Young authors affectiontely began to call him "the Pope of Russell Square." They were not describing his religious views, but rather his sedate and serious manner, as well as his increasingly important role as a mentor to younger writers. These ranged from Marianne Moore and Lawrence Durrell to Charles Williams, the circle of W. H. Auden, and Djuna Barnes. Eliot was often secretly generous financially to fellow poets and he brought them his writer's understanding along with careful editing. He might pencil in a suggestion in the margin, but he sought only to clarify an author's ideas, not change them.

Visitors described him sitting hunched over (partly a mannerism and partly an indication of his increasing emphysema), speaking slowly and hesitantly. His secretary Anne Ridler, also a poet, said that Eliot gave dictation fluently. He liked people to stand up for themselves, and hated having to read poetry that was imitation Eliot.

During the middle '30s Eliot continued to try to keep *The Criterion* featuring a variety of views. In addition, he lent a hand to keep alive A. R. Orage's *New English Weekly*, which now was edited by Philip Mairet. Mairet had help from Maurice Reckitt, who had also contributed to Chesterton's *G.K.'s Weekly* and had his own periodical called *Christendom*. Both men became friends of Eliot's. Eliot continued to give talks on the BBC about Christianity and the social order, and wrote for or served on editorial boards of other periodicals like *Time and Tide*.

The success of *Murder in the Cathedral* had confirmed his determination to stay in the theater to write plays that contemporary audiences would accept. Having captured the religious market, Eliot wanted to reach across class lines to appeal on different levels of meaning to a broader spectrum of society. He was also beginning work on a new poem, which was to form the first movement of *Four Quartets*.

The poem opened with some verses about the nature of time, which Martin Browne had cut out of *Murder in the Cathedral* because they slowed down the action. But the main image of the poem was suggested by a visit Eliot made with his old Boston friend Emily Hale to the house called "Burnt Norton" in Gloucestershire near Chipping Campden. After Eliot left America, he and Emily had corresponded, and he sent her some of his work in progress. Hale taught speech and drama at various women's colleges, and her favorite students and friends occasionally were read new Eliot poems.

As a result, some critics have tried to prove that Emily Hale was the "girl he left behind," the model for "La Figlia Che Piange" and the "hyacinth girl" in *The Waste Land*, as well as several other characters in his plays. As has been noted, the Hale correspondence is locked up until A.D. 2020 in the Princeton Library, so the story, if there is one, will have wait until then. In any case, Eliot was married until 1949, and despite

hard work and an austere existence, even critical observers like Virginia
Woolf felt that he was finally living the way he wanted to.

During 1936 Eliot also visited Little Gidding in East Anglia, which
had been the home of Nicholas Ferrar and his seventeenth-century
Christian community. Then in 1937 he went to East Coker in Somerset,
where his Eliot ancestors had lived before going to America. Together
with New England, these places were to be the other major images in
Four Quartets. Places and occasions had always made a deep impression on Eliot, who wrote a friend that at such times he felt removed
from everything that made him "an Eliot"—either the Boston Puritan
or the London writer.

As Eliot continued to be busy and productive, more and more he
recognized how necessary a "commonplace" or workaday life was to
artists if they were to get their work done. He began to sound very
much like C. S. Lewis, who needed the "ordinariness" of an uneventful
existence to accomplish anything worthwhile. Both men were establishing a pattern of living that also embodied their Christian convictions about the sacramental nature of work. Dorothy L. Sayers was to
write a great deal about the sanctity of the "right kind of work," but,
perhaps because she was a woman and expected to do society's daily
tasks, she had less patience than either Eliot or Lewis with the ordinary
demands of others.

Increasingly, too, Eliot was involved with people whom he had met
through church leaders like Bishop Bell. Some of them were seeking
ways of formulating a Christian point of view on politics in order to ar-
ticulate a Christian social conscience. Eliot's conversion had introduced
him to both the Negative and Affirmative Ways of Christian living.
Any personal bias toward the more monastic way was being countered
by his increasing sense of being part of a worshiping community, with
the responsibility of helping that community maintain Christian values
for the world at large.

This growing concern, or mission, appeared in essays he wrote as
well as in *Criterion* editorials. For example, in a 1935 essay, "Religion
and Literature," Eliot now insisted that literary criticism was complete
only when it was based on an ethical and theological standpoint, because literary greatness cannot be judged by literary standards alone.

Eliot then described three kinds of religious literature. The first was the Bible itself, although he disapproved of "parasites" who loved the Bible as literature. The second was devotional poetry or prose like that written by George Herbert or Gerard Manley Hopkins. Modern critics usually said that these artists had left out "real life," and Eliot agreed that they were minor poets compared to a Dante.

The third group of religious writers wrote "propaganda," or literature meant to speak to a world where religion and literature were no longer related. Ironically, his prime example was G. K. Chesterton's *Man Who Was Thursday* and the Father Brown stories. Eliot felt that this kind of work, when written by a writer less talented than Chesterton, had only a negative effect on the pagan world.

What Eliot wanted to create, therefore, was "unconsciously" Christian literature or writing that used the common denominator of human behavior to make the connection between literature and religion. He wanted to affect the reader as a whole human being, morally and aesthetically. He did feel that modern civilization had learned very little from its ancestors, but he said that his so-called pessimism over the return of the "barbarians" was really a fight against a secularism that did not understand the primacy of the supernatural over the natural life.

As Eliot built himself a new way of life, rooted in the daily practice of communal Christian worship, study, and prayer, world peace and prosperity were being thrown away by the League of Nations. The faint-hearted democracies sought no confrontations with dictators, and a postwar mood of pacifism had infected English intellectuals, led by the universities, the Labour Party, and groups like Canon "Dick" Sheppard's Peace Pledge Union.

Then in 1936 Hitler broke the Treaty of Versailles by taking over the Rhineland, Mussolini took Ethiopia, and together they formed the Axis alliance. That same year the Spanish Civil War began, secretly supported by Russia and Germany. This war became a crusade for the younger leftists in England, many of whom, breaking with their elders, went to fight against Franco. Like Jacques Maritain in France, Eliot took the unpopular view that it was better for intellectuals to remain neutral than to sign up for either side. In this position he was to be joined by George Orwell, who, disillusioned by the war in Spain, also spoke out against extremists and fanatics on both sides.

In England, the popular George V had been the living embodiment of the qualities Eliot, Williams, and Sayers, as well as Shaw and Chesterton, admired in the monarchy. He personified order, continuity, faith, and duty. In 1936 George V died and was succeeded by his son Edward VIII. Edward, unable to marry the divorced woman he loved, soon reluctantly abdicated in favor of his brother, the duke of York, who became George VI.

Many intellectuals thought Edward VIII had been railroaded by church, state, and the press. But, as Dorothy L. Sayers remarked, the king's dilemma was like that of Aeneas, the prince of Troy. Aeneas had a choice: either to marry Dido or to found Rome, but his destiny was not to do both. Eliot did not speak out editorially on the issue except to suggest that there is a difference between the office and the man.

In June 1936 G. K. Chesterton, worn out by his never-ending struggle to maintain his brother's independent weekly, suddenly died. As a familiar London newspaper columnist and a friendly voice heard on the BBC, Chesterton was mourned worldwide by millions who no longer shared his Christianity. Paradoxically, it fell to Eliot as the leading literary voice in London to speak Chesterton's *Nunc Dimittis*.

Eliot wrote an obituary for *The Tablet* and for his own *Criterion*. Typically for Eliot, he did not become personal or sentimental, nor did he try to judge Chesterton as an artist. Instead he praised Chesterton for his "lonely moral battle" against the times and for his bold combination of "genuine conservativism, genuine liberalism, and genuine radicalism." Chesterton, he declared, had done more than any man in his age to maintain the "existence of the important (Christian) minority in the modern world."

Coming so soon after the 1935 publication of *After Strange Gods*, in which Eliot had publicly picked up the torch Chesterton had been holding aloft, those comments were not meant to be derogatory. On the contrary, Eliot was publicly proclaiming that, whatever their differences about the way verse should be written, he knew himself to be one of Chesterton's heirs. In her introduction to Chesterton's *Surprise*, Dorothy L. Sayers also praised GKC as the "Christian liberator" of their generation, and C. S. Lewis described his discipleship in his autobiography, *Surprised by Joy*.

In another kind of Chestertonian discipleship, Eliot and some associates at *The Criterion* and the *New English Weekly* were exploring an economic *via media* between socialism and capitalism called "Social Credit." This was the economic theory of the Chandos Group, who met at the Chandos Restaurant in St. Martin's Lane.

Eliot acknowledged that Social Credit's ideas were close to Chesterton's Distributism, which sought a wider distribution of goods and property, and insisted that socially and economically "small is beautiful." Although Eliot did not agree with some Social Credit ideas, like the abolition of banks and the distribution of credit evenly throughout the population, he considered that economic problems like unemployment were moral at heart and must be addressed. He was also against a material culture which depended on people buying things they did not want. But Eliot never became an outspoken extremist like Ezra Pound, who carried his passionate economic theories to America, hoping to teach FDR what was wrong with the New Deal.

Eliot saw that most intellectuals were not really neutral or impartial about social issues; often they desired power more than justice. Two examples were to be found in education and land. More money would not solve the problems of the former, while the right relationship between city and country was crucial but difficult to define. On the other hand, Eliot was adamant in his editorials about the need for freedom from censorship. For him, censorship represented state control of something that should be governed "domestically" by custom.

During 1936 Eliot was asked to serve on an archbishop's committee to plan a conference at Oxford on Church, Community, and State. In 1937 he attended the conference and read a paper on the "Ecumenical Nature of the Church and Its Responsibility towards the World." He also took part in meetings at Lambeth that led to the establishment of the British branch of the World Council of Churches, of which Bishop Bell was to become a leader.

In February 1937 Eliot gave a talk on the BBC, "The Church's Message to the World," which was later appended to *The Idea of a Christian Society*. In it Eliot told his radio audience that a certain tension between church and state was desirable, but it was not always easy to distinguish between the church and the world. The church, however, did not exist solely for morality, which was only a means to an end, nor was the church only for the elect.

He did not think that Christianity demanded any particular form of government, conservative, liberal, or revolutionary. But he feared that a neutral society would not last long while a pagan society was an abomination to democracy. The church needed to say what was wrong, basing its criticism on Christian principles of personal and social order, but to do that there must be a Christian community studying and supporting those ideals. This was the germ of Eliot's idea of a Christian society. His view shared many similarities with Charles Williams's "Company," or "Order of the Co-inherence."

During 1938, evidently at the suggestion of her doctor, Vivien Eliot was examined by two other doctors, and then was committed to a private mental hospital called Northumberland House. She lived there until she died in 1949. Although he shared financial responsibilty for her with Vivien's brother Maurice, Eliot could not have signed the committal papers because they were legally separated. Two other relatives or friends did so—possibly her mother, or her brother and his wife. Much later, Maurice felt terribly guilty and tried to distance himself from the whole affair and blame Eliot. But when Vivian did try, unsuccessfully, to leave the mental hospital, there was no one who could or would take care of her outside. Her situation was undoubtedly a major source of Eliot's sense of sin, which was to be reflected in some of his next creative work.

By 1938 Eliot had published *Essays Ancient and Modern* and *Collected Poems 1909-1935*. The essays included those from *For Lancelot Andrewes* as well as more recent ones like "Religion and Literature." The poetry collection included the new poem "Burnt Norton."

Eliot's work was given a mixed reception. While most critics were still prepared to listen to what Eliot said about individual writers, or to admire his poems, they showed hostility or bewilderment at his attempt to establish a "Christian poetics" or to discuss a "Christian polity." In both cases they either argued that Eliot's "traditional approach" was outdated, or they described classical Christianity as if it were Eliot's personal heresy, ignoring his daily immersion in mainstream Christianity through the services of *The Book of Common Prayer*.

Meanwhile, although he had been asked to write other religious plays like *Murder in the Cathedral*, Eliot was determined to write a verse play with modern characters, not a period or "Gothick" piece. But the creative transition he made from *Ash-Wednesday* through *Murder in the Cathedral* to *The Family Reunion* is clear.

The protagonist of *The Family Reunion*, Harry Monchensey, is neither saint nor hero, although like Thomas he is a martyr (or witness) to the supernatural. Unlike *Murder in the Cathedral*, with its liturgical elements, where the real drama is in the choruses, the action of *The Family Reunion* is centered in the protagonist, who makes the "turning" (or conversion) Eliot had described in *Ash-Wednesday*.

Eliot followed his usual habit of "correlating" his work with a tradition of Western Civilization. *The Family Reunion* was based on the Greek myth of Orestes, who was pursued by the Furies for the murder of his mother, but in this play there was no real murder, only the suggestion that for the Christian to contemplate a crime was to commit it. Eliot's invisible Furies do nothing except appear twice to the hero. To give a modern twist, Eliot used the thriller framework of Dostoyevsky's *Crime and Punishment*, in which what happened to the victim must be discovered.

Eliot's plot has a triple structure. The hero searchs for expiation, his mother plans to reestablish the old family traditions, and the other relatives try to detect any real guilt or murder. This complicated structure also has an element missing from Eliot's more recent work; the play is full of his irony, wit, and humor.

The Family Reunion proved to be a kind of spiritual autobiography, in which anyone familiar with Eliot's life can catch personal echoes. Eliot tried to show the protagonist discovering a meaning to existence, which reintegrated his personality and changed the direction of his life. Harry believed he had killed his wife and was searching for a way of expiation. The detection plot reveals the dead wife's unstable, obsessive temperament, her endless emotional claims on her husband, and her nervous anxiety at his failure to satisfy her demands.

In the course of the play, Harry has to discover his role in his family. Harry's aristocratic English family is run by a matriarch who has assembled the entire clan to celebrate her birthday and the return of the heir. She plans to keep Harry at home and marry him to the girl he left behind. Some critics have seen in this part of the plot a version of Eliot's return to his own family after his marriage, as well as his subsequent refusal to "stay home" in America.

The action of the play takes place in a Jamesian, ghost-filled, English country estate called Wishwood. By returning home, Harry was able to reexplore old family relationships and face his own sense of guilt. Suddenly he could see the Furies, who had been following him. Like Francis Thompson's pursuing "Hound of Heaven," Eliot's Furies represent the jealous God whom the hero must face to discover that He is Love more than they represent classic avengers.

Once seen, the Furies offer Harry a new life, where he can expiate the family (or mankind's) "curse," which is not murder but original sin, and work out his own salvation. But to follow them, Harry must leave home again. In leaving, he expresses no remorse for his wife's death and his departure kills his mother.

Many critics and audiences could not comprehend Harry's "release" from remorse or his decision to leave home as a triumph for anyone. As Dorothy L. Sayers explained, *The Family Reunion* came close to being a "Christian tragedy" because it was only when the protagonist was stripped of his last "worldly holding" that the curse of sin was lifted, making him free to pursue a new and positive course of action.

In addition, the play itself was baffling to an audience with its chorus of bewildered, amusing family members, its "invisible" Furies wearing evening dress, and its major actors like Harry, his aunt Agatha who is principal of a woman's college, and Mary his cousin, who deliver set pieces like operatic arias. It did not work well on Eliot's different levels of meaning, and many people agreed with one of the Monchensey aunts, who said she did not understand a single thing that was happening. The Monchensey family also sounded and behaved more like the proper Bostonians of John P. Marquand's play *The Late George Apley* than like ancient Greeks or modern Englishmen. But the verse itself is some of Eliot's best, leading him naturally to the splendor of his next great work, *Four Quartets*.

Later, in a lecture on "Poetry and Drama" delivered at Harvard in 1951, Eliot approached *The Family Reunion* in a mood of high comedy. For example, Eliot cheerfully explained that he had never solved the staging of the Furies, who either became "Greek goddesses or modern spooks." He felt that the best solution was not to have them visible at all. Eliot added that the play had never decided if it was the tragedy of a possessive mother, trying to maintain home and hearth, or the salvation of a son who comes home only to leave again. He insisted, tongue in cheek, that his sympathy was all with the mother because the son was an insufferable prig. Several critics promptly announced that all Eliot heroes are insufferable prigs, clearly being chips off their creator's block. Dramatically speaking, in spite of the excellence of its poetry, The Family Reunion is not a perfect play—but it works more effectively when heard or seen than when merely read.

Perhaps the most interesting thing about The Family Reunion is that its atmosphere resembles the double world of time and eternity found in Charles Williams's theological thrillers like The Place of the Lion and Descent into Hell. By the late '30s, Eliot and Williams had known one another casually for over ten years, having met at one of Lady Ottoline Morrell's literary parties, and then lunched with mutual friends.

Williams had written to congratulate Eliot on Ash-Wednesday. He said their great-grandchildren would call it great poetry. Then he incautiously asked Eliot if there were some special meaning to the "three leopards" that "one would perhaps be happier for recognizing."

In turn, Eliot had congratulated Williams on the awareness of spiritual reality in The Place of the Lion. Eliot then asked Williams to review E. M. W. Tillyard's book on Milton for The Criterion. He said he was curious to know Williams's opinion about it, thus beginning the process by which Williams changed Eliot's (and C. S. Lewis's) views on Milton. Eliot was also much impressed by Williams's Canterbury play, Thomas Cranmer, which had followed Murder in the Cathedral, and wrote Williams he wanted to talk about it at "lunch . . . tea . . . dinner . . . supper—or breakfast at any time."

By 1940 Eliot was writing to "My dear Charles" to tell him that one of Williams's most important functions in life was to instill sound doctrine into people as he had tried to do in The Family Reunion. Eliot was also publishing some of Williams's best work at Faber & Faber and encouraging his poetry writing.

Anne Ridler, who knew them both well, wrote that in many ways their literary worlds did not overlap; much of their association was related to Church of England matters. But their relationship was sufficiently friendly for Eliot to tease Williams. He wrote to ask if Williams were going to be called "The Blessed Charles" while still alive. For his part, Williams was well aware that he was envious of Eliot's far greater fame as a poet and confessed as much to Eliot, who, Ridler says, responded with an amusing poem as yet unpublished.

Just before World War II began, as if sensing that the world was in need of comic relief, Eliot published a collection of poems written for his young cousins and godchildren, called *Old Possum's Book of Practical Cats*. Possum of course was one of Eliot's aliases like "the elephant" or the "Aged Eagle." That appelation dated back to Ezra Pound, who bestowed it on Eliot because of his ability to "play possum" to avoid being hurt.

These poems chronicle the adventures of a series of cats and dogs. They are nonsense verse of a high order, belonging with Edward Lear's work in the great English tradition. Their recent electric metamorphosis in the psychedelic Andrew Lloyd Webber musical *CATS!* with its spectacular staging has made these poems immortal in a way that would please their author. His second wife Valerie Eliot recognized that to be author of the book of one of the most successful stage shows ever produced would have made Tom's cup run over.

The poems themselves describe well-known felines like Growltiger, Old Deuteronomy, The Rum Tum Tugger, and Macavity: The Mystery Cat, who is clearly derived from Moriarty, the arch enemy of Sherlock Holmes. A lifelong love of and understanding of cats was an Eliot characteristic, as shown in the episode when Eliot met the Levys' cat "Lord Peter Wimsey" and sat sneaking Wimsey bits of shrimp during lunch. The cat's name was appropriate, too, since Dorothy L. Sayers's shared Eliot's love of cats, housing and feeding dozens herself.

Both the poems and their dedication showed Eliot's affection for children. His young American cousin Teddy Welch, who took refuge from the adults under the dining table with cousin Tom, received a personal copy of *Old Possum's Book of Practical Cats*, carefully inscribed

"for Teddy Welch by (T.S. Eliot

(Old Possum

(Cousin Tom"

Ted Welch prefers the poem about the Magician Cat, "Mr. Mistoffelees," because he is a practicing magician.

In January 1939 Eliot stopped publishing *The Criterion*, saying he felt stale as editor and the times were out of joint. The Munich agreement between Adolph Hitler and Neville Chamberlain had depressed him terribly by convincing him that Western civilization had given away its birthright for "peace in our time." In spite of his action, in his last *Criterion* editorial Eliot agreed with C. S. Lewis who that fall preached to the entering Oxford undergraduates that "business as usual," especially in the arts, was more important than ever.

Eliot's contrasting emotions show that, at the time World War II began, he shared the sense of failure felt by Lewis and Sayers, and also felt their driving need to reexamine Christendom's roots in hopes of resurrecting it. For them all, World War II was a watershed, moving them into more active roles as Christian spokesmen and opening up wider and different audiences.

Eliot gave the Boutwood Foundation lectures at Corpus Christi College, Cambridge, in March 1939, speaking to a small roomful of chilly listeners. Those lectures were published that October with the title *The Idea of a Christian Society*. Throughout there are echoes of Charles Williams's image of the City as the place of co-inherence, requiring mutual exchange at the intersection of time and place. Eliot's less sociological exposition of Williams's City was to appear in *Four Quartets*.

In *The Idea of a Christian Society*, Eliot tried to describe the kind of Christian society that needed to be built in "England's green and pleasant land." Eliot noted that much of what he said about a Christian society was based on discussions he had with a group called The Moot. Eliot's lectures and subsequent book also had a great deal in common with Sayers's wartime book *Begin Here*.

Eliot believed that the disappearance of Christianity would mean the end of Western civilization; dictatorships could stop its decline only artificially. Urbanization and industrialization had destroyed the individual. By replacing the Liberal belief in progress with (welfare) "statism," statism had taken away an individual's private life in the name of democracy.

Fascism was clearly pagan, but England was still "Christian," although heading toward a "neutral" state of being in which pluralism would be the rule. The only thing to do was to try to rebuild England as a Christian society, so Eliot tried next to define what that would be.

In his opinion, a Christian society should not accept Liberalism's belief that religious views were a private affair because it was hard to be a Christian in a non-Christian society whose institutions did not transmit Christian traditions. By tolerating all beliefs, soon the only Christians left would be adult converts, who would be a persecuted minority. Eliot felt therefore that the only hope for Western society to continue being creative was for it to become Christian again.

He then continued with his argument from *After Strange Gods*, that the arts resulted from "continuity and coherence in literature" which was created by education. Eliot wanted to see a distinction made between the educated and the uneducated, together with consistent study of fewer works. Echoing Chesterton in *What's Wrong with the World*, Eliot said that a country's educational system was more significant than its form of government because society used education to impose its beliefs.

Eliot then discussed reestablishing the parish as the local unit of government to counteract suburban sprawl and the loss of community. The ideal community would include all classes, and would be religious and social in focus, ruled by a Christian "elite" (or order), made up of lay and clerical people whose role was to educate the values of the ordinary citizen.

In his last lecture Eliot tackled industrial urbanization. To Eliot, religion meant living with the natural world, but the modern idea of nature had become so distorted that celibacy was called "unnatural" and limiting family size was "natural." Industrialization deformed human beings and exhausted our natural resources, and our descendents would pay for our prosperity.

For Eliot, the wrong attitude toward nature was the wrong attitude toward God. Only with effort and discipline did society gain material knowledge and power without losing its spiritual power and knowledge. Man needed to see the world again the way the Christian fathers had seen it, recovering "the sense of religious fear, so that it may be overcome by religious hope."

CHAPTER NINE

War
1939 – 1945

WORLD WAR II BROKE OUT ON SEPTEMBER 1, 1939, WHEN GERMANY
failed to respond to the ultimatum of Great Britain and France to leave
Poland. After that, Germany continued its conquest of continental
Europe and country after country fell. Busy getting *The Idea of a Christian Society* into print, Eliot's reaction to a "catastrophe that now included war" was to prepare for battle. He was against pacifism, fearing
a new Dark Ages if the Axis won, but he also spoke out publicly against
punishing conscientious objectors. As G. K. Chesterton had said about
the Boer War, Eliot felt that a statement like "My country, right or
wrong," was like saying "my mother, drunk or sober." Instead, Eliot
tried to be a conscientious critic and to work toward a Christian plan
for the postwar world.

For Eliot, like his middle-aged contemporaries, the war also meant
carrying an extra load of work under difficult circumstances and trying
to find ways of "being useful." On the home front, C. S. Lewis prepared

for London evacuees and covered the Kilns windows with blackout curtains. Dorothy L. Sayers volunteered to help the Ministry of Information and began to knit helmets and stockings. Charles Williams faced the prospect of leaving London with the Oxford University Press. Eliot trained to be an air raid warden by putting out practice fires in Kensington Gardens.

For him, as for Lewis and Sayers, World War II was a period when their evangelism became really important to their society. All of them spoke regularly as Christians on the BBC, and Eliot became more deeply involved in the ecumenical movement (his interest was a result of the failure of communication that had caused the war). The fruit of their wartime experiences of fear, monotony, and overwork was to be some of their best work.

As a result of the 1937 Oxford Conference and the 1938 Lambeth meetings, Eliot had begun to attend The Moot, begun by Dr. J. H. Oldham, who organized the Oxford Conference. Oldham also got Philip Mairet, who had belonged to the Chandos Group and was editing the *New English Weekly*, to begin the *Christian News Letter* with the help of Maurice Reckitt. During the war, Eliot helped edit both journals and contributed work to them, including the final three parts of *Four Quartets*.

The Moot was a group of Christian intellectuals and professional people who met several times a year from 1938 to 1947 to study and discuss the basic problems of a Christian society. Only about a dozen people came regularly. Among those involved at one time or another were Eliot and other writers like J. Middleton Murry, theologians like Christopher Dawson, Reinhold Niebuhr, and Paul Tillich, academics like Karl Mannheim and Michael Polanyi, churchmen like Rev. J. Lesslie Newbigin and Archbishop William Temple, politicians like Anthony Eden and Richard Crossman, and historians like R. H. Tawney and Arnold Toynbee. The Moot's membership represented Eliot's idea of a Christian elite.

By the time war broke out, Moot members were moving in different philosophical directions. Some, like Eliot, believed there was need for further intellectual exploration; others wanted to organize at once for collective action. But their understanding of the underlying problem was similar.

Karl Mannheim, for example, who was considered one of The Moot's activists, described the modern world in terms similar to Eliot's *Waste Land*. In *Diagnosis of Our Time*, Mannheim said that the "despiritualization" of modern life came from its lack of authentic "paradigmatic" experiences (Eliot's unattended moments) which let individuals rank experience in some kind of order. The result was the evaporation of those images that objectify a people's faith and provide its moral imagination. By contrast, Eliot was already convinced that the Church itself could and should provide a basis for restoring the City, or a sense of Christian community.

The interchange promoted by The Moot between individuals of different backgrounds and activities not only developed a deep sense of kinship and loyalty among the members, but it was tremendously fruitful for Eliot's own development. The Moot continued to meet when possible during the war but it was never able to agree on a social agenda. It finally ceased to exist when Karl Mannheim died. This was just after the Labour government had taken office, charged with bringing in the postwar "new world." Many of the ideas explored by The Moot appeared in Eliot's "answer" to the welfare state, *Notes Toward the Definition of Culture*, which was published in 1949.

In the meantime, the war was going badly for England. By June 1940 what was left of the British forces in France had to be rescued from Dunkirk, and the Battle of Britain began. The tiny RAF fought for control of the English Channel to prevent an invasion. Winston Churchill took over as prime minister, offering the English only "blood, toil, tears, and sweat."

Life in Kensington became impossibly tiring for Eliot, who had firewatch duty two nights a week. By September when the nightly bombing of London began, Eliot had moved to Shamley Green near Richmond, where he was a "paying guest" in the home of writer Hope Mirrlees, her mother, and aunt. Eliot found life with them comfortable and even enjoyed the old aunt who cadged his cigarettes.

Eliot commuted to work in London three days a week, spending the nights in Hampstead with the Fabers who had an air raid shelter. The other four days he worked at Richmond. The "hellish" trips that appear in *Four Quartets* reflect both his wartime traveling to London and his trips across the island to give talks and take part in conferences.

Along with his regular work, home-front responsibilities, editorial jobs, and meetings, Eliot also chaired a "books across the sea" project. His job was to make available to the London public scarce American and English books on postwar reconstruction, education, and cultural institutions.

Since the London theaters had been closed, Eliot returned to writing poetry. He later told an interviewer that he could write a poem in pieces without worrying so much about its continuity, which suited the difficult circumstances under which he wrote. But it was only as he worked on "East Coker," the second poem of *Four Quartets*, that he realized that it could be given the same five-part structure as "Burnt Norton." At this point he decided to repeat the themes from the other poem in a manner similar to the composition of a musical quartet by Beethoven, whose work he admired.

Eliot's experience writing the verse of *The Family Reunion* helped to make *Four Quartets* a poetic masterpiece. In the completed poem, the subject of the play finally found a satisfactory artistic expression; in the third movement of each poem, there is a "turning," which was expressed lyrically in the fourth movement, then was resolved in the fifth or final movement.

In these poems, as in other things written by Eliot at the same time, there was a progression from his tragic sense of human solitude toward an acceptance of life lived in society. The final poem, "Little Gidding," combined and transcended both tragic and comic visions, suggesting that they would coinhere within the true Christian community.

What Eliot also sought to describe was the relationship between time and eternity, and *Four Quartets* was a meditation on St. Augustine's *Confessions*. For St. Augustine, time was rooted in the imagination. The past existed in the mind's ability to recollect; the future existed in its expectations. The present came from the imagination's fusing of the memory of the past and the anticipation of the future. St. Augustine's approach was fundamentally biblical; there, all times are God's, and their significance comes from man's response to God's purpose.

As Eliot had explained in "Tradition and the Individual Talent," the modern literary trend had been toward "mythologizing," or reaching back to timeless archetypes to free man from the present. This "timelessness" was reflected in literature's filmlike juxtapositions and confusion. Modern life was shown not as a pilgrimage or journey but as circular and confused. Eliot's contemporaries like Yeats and Joyce were still trying to build Yeats's "Byzantium," a City above and beyond time's filthy load, freed of what Simone Weil called the "superstition of chronology." Like primitive man, these writers hoped by repeated patterns or cycles to be saved from time's duration and end.

Eliot disagreed with their solution. Eliot, too, was seeking to free man from a sense of linear progress, but he accepted the fact that human life was irrevocably conditioned by time and history. In his first quartet, "Burnt Norton," Eliot had said that "Only through time is time conquered." For Eliot all time was equally distant from eternity, and both kinds of time—chronos and kairos—coexisted. The one great intersection of time and eternity had occurred at the Incarnation, an irreversible and unrepeatable event, which had redeemed time for the human race. Eliot felt that the saints experienced the intersection of *chronos* and *kairos* continually, while the rest of us know eternity only in "unattended moments" of grace, which must be followed by "prayer, observance, discipline, thought and action." Mankind must work to redeem the time by taking the right action—responsible involvement with the community—here and now.

As a confession of faith, *Four Quartets* also completed the process of Eliot's artistic transition from a poet who wrote dramatic monologues, hiding behind a variety of voices, to one who spoke directly, making a personal statement of belief. Still, as Eliot said, a poet does not persuade people to believe; he teaches them what it feels like to believe.

Four Quartets is a modern religious meditation which has become a classic of Anglican spirituality because he reaffirmed the Incarnational faith of Richard Hooker and Lancelot Andrewes. Although Eliot lived in Auden's "Age of Anxiety," where death or sin paled beside the threat of meaninglessness, he affirmed that all human beings are occasionally "surprised by joy" and can live within its context in the church's word and sacraments.

Each of the four quartets was associated with the special place indicated by its title. "Burnt Norton," for example, came from Eliot's visit with Emily Hale to that house, but in the lyrical fourth movement Eliot also remembered a walk to Avesham Church made while visiting Brother George Every at Kelham.

Four Quartets also contained an ongoing meditation by the poet on the craft of writing. His concern with the difficulties of saying what he truly meant form an interesting counterpoint to Dorothy L. Sayers's discussion of the same problem in *The Mind of the Maker*.

Finally, *Four Quartets* was a monument to the friendship between Eliot and John Hayward. Hayward read the work in progress, playing the critical yet sympathetic role of editor that Ezra Pound had played with *The Waste Land* and Martin Browne with *Murder in the Cathedral*. Eliot acknowledged Hayward's help when the entire poem was published in 1943.

Eliot did not begin the second poem, "East Coker" until late 1939, but he completed it by early 1940. East Coker, the English village from which his ancestors had sailed for America, was much the same three hundred years later. The poem expressed his personal sense of continuity and celebrated England at a time when it was threatened by German invasion. The poem's basic theme is the same as *The Family Reunion* and *The Idea of a Christian Society*: suffering can provide salvation for individuals and society, if they will be still and wait on the Lord.

Eliot invoked his sixteenth-century ancestor, Sir Thomas Elyot, then recalled rustic revels in the field nearby with its ancient stone circle. But harmony with the natural world did not help the poet find an answer in the past. The crucial section of the poem is the lyric fourth movement, where Christ, the wounded surgeon, allows us to meet him through his broken body and blood. In part five, the aging poet still struggles with words. The important thing is trying. Where it leads is not the poet's business, but old men must still be explorers.

"East Coker" was published separately at Easter 1940. By late 1940 Eliot had completed "The Dry Salvages," the third poem of *Four Quartets*, and by February 1940 it too had been published in the *New English Weekly*. In this poem Eliot returned to his American roots and the scenes of his youth, describing the "strong brown god" of the Mississippi and the rocky New England coastline.

Awash in the contemporary sense of time as flux, or drifting wreckage, the sea (which is primeval time) is all about us. Time is both destroyer and preserver, a source of primitive terror whose moments of agony and vision come from our place between time and eternity. We share the experience of those moments with our ancestors, and they are easier to understand in the agony of others, especially that of Christ.

Then in a kind of doxology, the bell on the submerged rocks rings to warn us and ask a response. The bell is the Angelus, reminding us of the Annunciation and giving us hope of the Incarnation. The Annunciation and the Incarnation unite time and eternity to save us from drifting and drowning. They allow us to "fare forward" with hope.

In the third movement, yet another Eliot journey, the passengers will not be the same when they disembark, but they must live in the present, for where they are going is where they already are. The fourth movement is a lyrical prayer to Our Lady, the handmaiden of the Lord, "Queen of Heaven," and Stella Maris, to whom the sailors pray. Eliot later told William Turner Levy that, as he wrote, he had been thinking of a church he had seen high above the harbor at Marseilles.

The last movement talks of how men try to learn from the past and foresee the future—all but the saints, who try to apprehend the Incarnation, where time and the timeless intersect. The rest of us have to live with "hints and guesses."

By the time "The Dry Salvages" was published at Easter 1941, Eliot's heavy schedule and exhaustion from wartime living were making him suffer almost chronic ill health. Acute attacks of bronchial disease, aggravated by his incessant smoking, became a pattern for the rest of his life. But he kept his professional schedule as busy as ever.

The Archbishop of York's Conference on the Life of the Church and the Order of Society, known as the Malvern Conference, was one of the many religious conferences where Eliot helped shape the apologetics of the Church of England in the postwar world. Held at Malvern in 1941, it reflected the participants' wish to define what was meant by a Christian society, as well as their strong sense of responsibility for the fact that war had broken out again. These Church of England members all felt disillusioned by the postwar policies of their youth, but also had a lack of conviction about the Allies' concept of "total victory."

The convenor was Archbishop William Temple, who shortly afterward became Archbishop of Canterbury. For three jam-packed days in January 1941, Dorothy L. Sayers and Eliot were among the ten speakers, nine of whom were laypersons, who presented papers. Sayers was the only woman.

There was a full agenda for the twenty-three bishops, eight deans and provosts, twenty-one canons, and over two hundred clergy and laity, about eighty of whom were women. Bishop Bell was present, as was Eliot's friend, Brother George Every from Kelham, and Father Patrick McLaughlin of the Church Union and Church Social Action, who shortly afterward persuaded Sayers, Eliot, and Charles Williams to join him in an effort at evangelical outreach at St. Anne's Soho.

Archbishop Temple's conference owed much to the Christian Socialist Movement of F. D. Maurice and Charles Kingsley, updated by the Anglo-Catholic Christian Social Union under Bishop Charles Gore and Conrad Noel, who were close friends of G. K. Chesterton. Most Malvern speakers subscribed to the Anglo-Catholic sacramental view of the world, and the conference officially adopted the Incarnation as the central principle governing any theory of men in society.

But their hope of achieving a purely Christian society was already under pressure from plans for the postwar welfare state. Sir Richard Acland, for example, an outspoken Labour MP, tried to get the conference to agree that socialism (or common ownership of the means of production) was the only Christian way. Inevitably, Acland got the most headlines, but under the leadership of the Archbishop, the conference agreed only that private ownership of a community's resources might be a stumbling block to a just society.

Eliot spoke on religious education. Education itself, which was related to his older preoccupation with culture, was becoming one of his main concerns. He was not in agreement with a recent statement by the country's religious leaders in favor of equal, state-controlled education for all. Instead he suggested the need for a specifically Christian doctrine of education. He did not lay down the law on what education should be, but urged the importance of establishing what it should include. He pointed out that education was the contemporary aspect of cultural tradition, by means of which each generation's awareness of its forebears' truths and experiences (its tradition) was perpetuated, but formal education was only a small part of education.

The modern tendency was to divide education compartmentally by subjects, while removing any sectarian restrictions on what was taught. The result was to promote what today is known as secular humanism, or to reinforce obedience to the mindset of the Minister of Education. That kind of education, pushed to extremes, would create George Orwell's 1984. To counteract this, Eliot felt that unless a Christian doctrine of man was developed, including a doctrine of education, society would merely adapt its system of education to a changing world without either permanent principles of education or standards of quality.

In summing up his conference, Archbishop Temple said that it had tried to reestablish Christian principles in relation to the world of today. Malvern was especially concerned with the role of the church, hoping to stimulate discussion within the church as well as "put it on the map" for those who felt it lacked relevance.

In 1942 Archbishop Temple published a paperback, *Christianity and the Social Order*, which popularized the whole subject and sold over 150,000 copies. The same year, however, the blueprint for the postwar welfare state, the famous Beveridge Report, was published. It contained most of Sir Richard Acland's platform at Malvern: nationalizing industry, reforming and broadening education for a "classless" society, providing total health insurance and full employment.

As a Christian, Eliot was not in favor of governmental organization of society at the expense of the individual. By 1943, writing in the *Christian News Letter* using one of his favorite pen names, "Metoikos," or resident alien, Eliot criticized the Beveridge Plan. He was not convinced that socialism would end the exercise of power by some over others; therefore he preferred a society whose culture kept a healthy relationship with its religious values or "the natural law." Eliot's ideas on education were strikingly similar to C. S. Lewis's views in *The Abolition of Man*, published in 1943.

In line with his American political background, Eliot felt that the abuse of power was best prevented by maintaining a balance between major groups, but he still preferred a governing elite drawn from a social class accustomed by education and background to rule, not a meritocracy. This was not only the traditional English system, but it had been the situation in America during its early history.

During 1942 Eliot had flown secretly to Sweden with Bishop Bell to make contact with some Germans organized against Hitler. One of them was theologian Dietrich Bonhoeffer. But the English government did not respond to their initiative, and Bonhoeffer was later executed in Tegel Prison for treason.

Despite difficult wartime conditions, Eliot continued to travel about the country giving lectures. Many of them were later published in collections like *On Poetry and Poets* and *To Criticize the Critic*. For example, Eliot gave the annual W. P. Ker Memorial Lecture at Glasgow University in 1942. In this talk on "The Music of Poetry," given in memory of a famous Chaucer scholar, Eliot first discussed the poet as critic. Then he described the act of poetic creation, saying that poetry cannot be written by rules but needed a deeper, more subtle "imitation" that resulted from analyzing the style of good poets. For Eliot, the music of poetry comes from everyday language, so that every "revolution" in poetry is a return to ordinary speech. Like music, poetry's structure comes from rhythm and recurring themes. In composing poetry, Eliot said that he sometimes had a rhythm in mind before he had words.

Upon his election as president of the Classical Association at Cambridge, Eliot gave a talk on "The Classics and the Man of Letters." He refused to call himself a classicist, saying he was only a "man of letters," but he felt a classical education was needed because literature was not just a succession of great men, but a succession of men of letters influencing one another. Minor writers need a classical education to know their own past; that unity of culture gives writers a wider audience.

Eliot went on to note that many people do not care about European culture because it is Christian, but Christianity itself must have Latin and Greek scholarship to keep its intellectual vigor. Still, no system of education can create great faith or great literature because education is not the parent but only the child of culture.

By June 1942 Eliot had a working draft of the last of the *Four Quartets*, called "Little Gidding" after an isolated hamlet in East Anglia. In 1625 Anglo-Catholic Nicholas Ferrar and his mother had established there a family "conventual" life, based on the services of *The Book of Common Prayer*. Ferrar was well educated and well connected, but instead of a public career he chose to live a private life of prayer and good works. This was the kind of life that appealed to Eliot's deepest instincts as a variation on the Negative Way.

In Ferrar's lifetime Little Gidding became a shrine of Anglican piety, beloved of the poet George Herbert, and visited by King Charles I who may have come there after his last, lost battle. After Ferrar's death Little Gidding was brutally sacked by Cromwell's Parliamentary troops. The Hall was left derelect, but the tiny chapel was rebuilt early in the eighteenth century and Ferrar's tombstone stands there to mark his grave.

The poem describes Little Gidding as both a place of defeat of worldly hopes and a place where "prayer is valid." But instead of meditating on the past (history) as he had done in "The Dry Salvages," Eliot explored society's public actions and the sins we commit against one another, showing them against the backdrop of eternity.

Eliot had known that in writing *Four Quartets* he had taken on the "daunting task" of trying to tell about faith and hope and the eternal Word made flesh in time. He did not expect his public to accept all he wrote, but he saw the poet's role to be the prophet's task of truth telling. In each poem he had talked about the problem of words and meaning, but in this last poem he described what perfect writing was, where "every word is at home."

Eliot also tried to resolve the dilemma of time and eternity by reconciling them. Mankind cannot turn its back on the earthly Unreal City as he did in *The Waste Land*, nor deny the world to live in the eternal City of God as seen in *Ash-Wednesday*. There is value in the past, or in experience, but mankind must live in the present, where only "moments of vision" in the rose garden or the chapel at dusk give glimpses of eternity. When all is said and done, the whole duty of man is to pray.

"Little Gidding" was written under the shadow of war, and Eliot called it a "patriotic poem"—by which he meant its mood of sadness and pity, not of vainglory. During spring and summer 1942 London was bombed night after night for ten straight months. On May 10 alone, three thousand people were killed in air raids and Eliot felt London's destruction in his very soul. In this poem he confessed to a sense of physical decay and exhaustion. Some critics took this to prove that the entire poem was bleak and melancholy, without hope or grace, ignoring the fact that Eliot was also affirming the redemption of time by the Incarnation.

For him the chapel at Little Gidding was symbolic of the church, or Christendom. The poem's other image is fire, destructive and refining, experienced in both the terrifying dark dive of the bomber and the bright descent of the Pentecostal dove. Eliot's Pentecostal imagery in "Little Gidding" was greatly influenced by Charles Williams's *Descent of the Dove: A Short History of the Holy Spirit*, which had been published by Faber & Faber in 1939.

"Little Gidding" opens with Eliot's visit to the chapel. His original visit in 1936, when he had a powerful experience of the presence of God, was in the spring. It may have been during Holy Week, or possibly on Whitsunday. In the poem Eliot's prayer pilgrimage takes place in "the dark time of the year," the "midwinter spring," when there was no wind but a pentecostal fire and snow. (It was also the dark midpoint of the war.) The site of Little Gidding was at the "end of the world." But now, in England, Little Gidding was "nearest in time and place" to the intersection of time and the timeless moment when the dead may prophesy with fire.

In the second movement Eliot brings back the themes of his earlier poems. He speaks of the death and decay of the four elements of life: air, fire, earth, and water, remembered in burnt roses, dust, crumbling walls, dead sand, and water. The world is being destroyed, just like the city he sees during his early morning watch as air raid warden when the German bombers come.

On his patrol, the air raid warden poet meets a "familiar compound ghost," who is the "dead master." This visitation seems to be made up of Eliot's dead fellow poets. The meter, style, and setting all suggest Dante, but the poet's ghostly companion on his walk through London streets is not just Dante nor Dante's guide, Virgil.

Many other possibilities have been suggested. One is the older and wiser blind poet, John Milton, of *Paradise Regained*. Or it may be the poet Yeats; after Yeats's death in 1939 Eliot had called him the greatest poet of the age, although neither had agreed with the other's way of walking on earth.

The "Magus" could even be James Joyce, who had recently died, together with Shakespeare, speaking through Hamlet's father's ghost when met on the battlements of Elsinore. The figure reminds still others of Jonathan Swift or Dr. Samuel Johnson. Finally, the wise ghost may be Eliot's own resurrected self meeting his *Doppelgänger*, or the shade of Nicholas Ferrar who was so like Eliot. Eliot seems to have used a multitude of cultural memories to create his composite guide, and all these allusions may have been intended by him.

The two poets patrol the ghostly City (another powerful Williams image, dominant in Eliot's poetry since *The Waste Land*). They speak of their mutual task as poets to "purify the dialect of the tribe." Then the poet's ghostly companion warns him about the trials old age will bring and suggests that only through the discipline of the refining fire can a poet hope to join the everlasting dance of life. The all-clear sounds, and the ghost departs.

Eliot then follows the two Ways to reconcile them with the affirmation of medieval Dame Julian of Norwich that Love causes all things to happen, so that despite past and present destruction, "All manner of thing shall be well/By the purification of the motive/In the ground of our beseeching."

In the lyrical fourth movement, which many consider Eliot's best, the Holy Ghost dives down like a bomber, offering the City the choice of "pyre or pyre," or redemption from fire by fire. But the torment brought by the Nazi planes was devised by Love, and in the end, man's only choice is between loving himself or God.

The final movement of "Little Gidding" repeats the themes of the other three quartets. Eliot uses a line from another great medieval mystic, the anonymous author of *The Cloud of Unknowing*, to affirm his faith that the beginning is often the end, just as an end may make a beginning. History (or time) is the place where the Holy Spirit operates, but his work also makes the pattern, or moving dance, from moments out of time. Finally, Eliot returns to the chapel, where he does not merge the moments in the rose garden and the chapel, but holds them together to create one vision of reality.

"Little Gidding" was harder for Eliot to write than the other poems because he wanted it to be a recapitulation of the whole work. Then, afraid that the poem lacked a personal sense, Eliot reworked sections two and three, making more explicit references to his poetic role and his own melancholy and anger. It was not until September 1942 that Eliot sent John Hayward the last version, which was published in the *New English Weekly* that October.

The publication of *Four Quartets*, first separately, then together in 1943, made a deep impression on many people at that difficult time. Among them was Helen Gardner, who became a distinguished Eliot critic; she said that for her generation *Four Quartets* had been the "most significant literary experience of the . . . Second World War." She considered the poem to be the mature masterpiece of a poet whose work had modified and enriched the English poetic tradition. After him, she said, poets wrote differently.

Other critics like George Orwell said that *Four Quartets* had no "fresh literary impulses" because Eliot did not feel his faith, but merely assented to its dogmas. While Stephen Spender said that the poem made beautiful use of Eliot's auditory imagination, proving that Eliot wrote "by ear," he and others saw Eliot as unforgivably didactic, much like Dante. (A more appropriate parallel might be the meditations and sermons of Eliot's favorite seventeenth-century Anglican divines like Bishop Andrewes, Hooker, and Jewel.)

The issue of whether or not the poem reflects real religious emotion or only Eliot's intellectual assent to orthodox Christianity has reappeared recently as critics probe psychologically for autobiographical sources. Some insist that the poem proves that Eliot had neither a God nor a religion, but only internal personality conflicts deriving from his Puritan background and unsatisfactory relationship with his mother. Others still stumble over Eliot's expressed self-doubt and equivocation, which he faithfully tried to portray as aspects of a faith like Charles Williams's, whose patron saint was doubting St. Thomas. It seems more sensible to observe the life Eliot led and, as he suggested in his essay on Pascal, judge him by its fruits.

Eliot continued to repeat his message in his prose. In "The Social Function of Poetry" (1943) he said that poetry not only expressed the feelings of the race but prevented it from losing its language by letting it communicate with its past. He suggested that the problem of the modern age was not only an inability to believe what its forefathers believed, but to feel the way they did about their beliefs.

In spite of the grim wartime circumstances, Eliot's essays often have a quiet humor and genial tone that was lacking in his earlier, more strident work. They fit the image of the benign master craftsman and show that, settled in his habits and convictions, whatever skeptical or depressed moods he still suffered, Eliot was achieving and expressing serenity in his life and work.

During the war Eliot often went to Oxford. When he did he made a point of seeing Charles Williams, who had been exiled there with the Oxford University Press "for the duration." In that lovely gothic town, which he, like Eliot, found provincial, Williams still conformed to London mores by wearing dark City suits.

In the early '30s when they had first met, Williams had written that he did not understand Eliot's poetry but respected it. When Williams's *Taliessin through Logres* appeared in 1939, Eliot told Brother George Every and the young poet Anne Ridler that he found Williams's poetry difficult and not a success. But after he read *The Descent of the Dove* Eliot felt he understood the poetry far better.

Williams remarked that Eliot's landscape was his own but Eliot's poetic voice was always more like the voice of St. John the Baptist "than the croak of the lizard near at hand." Brother George Every, a friend to both men, commented that they were poets of very different kinds to start with. In spite of that, however, their verse came to have considerable similarity.

During 1942-43 Charles Williams completed *The Figure of Beatrice*, his study of Dante, for Faber & Faber. Eliot was the editor, and their shared admiration for Dante was a close bond between them. But Williams was annoyed when Eliot insisted that the opening chapter be rewritten because it was obscure—after C. S. Lewis had told him that it was the clearest thing that he, Williams, had ever written.

During his Oxford stay, Williams had begun to meet regularly with the Inklings, a group of Christians who met to talk and read their work in progress to one another. Like Sayers, Eliot never attended any Inkling meetings although he knew and read their work and was personally acquainted with most of them.

Neither the Inklings, Sayers, or Eliot lived like a Christian community or formed a clique. But it is just as misleading to suggest they had nothing in common, when they were all orthodox Christians in a pagan world with most of the intellectual community ranged against them. Christianty was one of the causes, not the result of their friendships; their common cause was Christian apologetics, growing out of an acute sense of social responsibility, heightened by war. They shared a devotion to Dante, whose *Divine Comedy* had also been addressed to a Christian Europe at war with itself. To some extent they were all heirs of Chesterton, showing his awareness of a timeless world and the historical process, intersected by the Incarnation, and they all shared an intellectual "passion" for Christianity.

The Inkling with whom Eliot did not have good relations was C. S. Lewis. Back at Oxford as a wounded veteran after World War I, Lewis had been personally antagonistic to Eliot's Modernist verse. Then in 1931 Lewis had submitted an essay on "The Personal Heresy in Criticism" to Eliot's *Criterion*. In it Lewis took issue with the critical approach of using an author's writing to discover his personality. He particularly accused two authors of "the personal heresy": T. S. Eliot on Dante and E. M. W. Tillyard on Milton.

Although Eliot himself was to suffer more than Lewis from such an approach, he was not convinced that the article was appropriate for his journal. Lewis's article sat at *The Criterion* for six months until he finally wrote a letter asking about it. Eliot, always too busy, delayed responding, and eventually turned Lewis's article down. Lewis promptly submitted it to *Essays and Studies*, where it was published in 1934, and started a debate with Tillyard.

During the '30s Lewis's continuing grudge against Eliot encouraged him and Tolkien in their academic refusal to deal with contemporary English poetry. Lewis even used Eliot's critical opinions on potential Oxford students to catch them out in literary heresy. Lewis continued to disapprove of Eliot even after Eliot's conversion in 1927, although Lewis, too, soon rejoined the Church. In his spiritual autobiography, *The Pilgrim's Regress*, published in 1934, Lewis described Eliot as Mr. Neo-angular, leader of an elitist intellectual clique bent on making Christianity into a "high-brow, Chelsea . . . fad."

But the two men kept an eye on each other's work. Sick with a bad cold over Christmas 1936, Lewis read and disliked Eliot's *Murder in the Cathedral*, in spite of the play's alliterative verse and subject matter. That same year Eliot gave his first talk on John Milton. Eliot announced that he found Milton unappealing as a person, however great he might be as a poet. By writing in a style so far from normal speech, Eliot felt that Milton had "deteriorated the language," and insisted Milton could be judged only by "a jury" of his poetic peers.

By 1942 Lewis had heard Charles Williams deliver his famous talk on Milton's *Comus* to an Oxford audience, and like Eliot, had read Williams's introduction to *The English Poems of John Milton*. Then Lewis himself gave a series of wartime lectures on Milton which were published as *A Preface to Paradise Lost*. Lewis dedicated the lectures to Charles Williams. He then proceeded to attack Eliot for suggesting that only the best contemporary, practicing poets could judge Milton's work. In Lewis's hands Eliot was either one of a too select "Invisible Church," who had declared themselves the best, or he was the sole judge of his right to call himself one of the best contemporary poets. Such poets might be able to explain whether or not writing poetry like Milton's was hard, but Lewis refused to allow Eliot or his poetic peers to be the only judges of whether or not reading Milton was worthwhile.

In the preface, Lewis did say that he agreed with Eliot "about matters of such moment that all literary questions are, by comparison, trivial," but he had attacked Eliot so strongly that he also sent Eliot a note of apology. There matters stood during most of the war, although Charles Williams continually threatened to introduce them to one another.

Apart from their shared interest in literature and their Christianity, the two men had a number of things in common. Both were shy men who had found themselves responsible for different but difficult women: Mrs. Moore and Vivien Eliot. Neither talked much about their "domestic" difficulties. Then unexpectedly, late in life, both men were to be happily married.

By 1943 the war began to turn in the Allies' favor, but Eliot's literary contemporaries, Yeats, James Joyce, and Virginia Woolf, were all dead. Ezra Pound was about to be imprisoned by the Americans for treason because of his wartime radio talks from Italy when the last German weapon, the terrifying and unpredictable buzz bombs, began landing in London.

One made a direct hit on the apartment on the top of Faber & Faber's building, making it necessary for Eliot to camp out in his office on his firewatching nights. Dorothy L. Sayers took refuge from those buzz bombs in her Witham shelter with a copy of Dante's *Inferno* and started to work on her translation.

Sayers and Eliot by now had both become involved with St. Anne's

House on Dean Street. When the Church of St. Anne's Soho was directly hit in 1940, only the bulbous, Russian-looking tower and the clergy
house remained standing. Sayers' ashes are now buried in the tower,
beneath her portrait and plaque installed by the Sayers Society.

St. Anne's location in the heart of the theater and foreign restaurant
district near Bloomsbury and the Inns of Court was ideal for an intellectual "outreach" program. With the permission of the Bishop of London, St. Anne's House was opened under the aegis of two priests, one
of whom, Father Patrick McLaughlin, had been at Malvern. Interested
in the relationship between the church, society, and culture, he brought
in Sayers and Eliot to speak on related topics.

That first year they both took part in a series of discussions held once
a week until mid-December on "Christian Faith and Contemporary
Culture." Other well-known figures who participated at various times
included the editor of *Time and Tide*, the director of the Victoria and
Albert Museum, Charles Williams, Rose Macaulay, Sir John Betjeman,
C. S. Lewis, Lord David Cecil, Iris Murdoch, Rebecca West, and Christopher Dawson. Among others who served on the advisory panel were
journalists Philip Mairet and Maurice Reckitt, J. H. Oldham and other
Moot members, Inkling Nevill Coghill, and Sayers.

The ongoing cultural discussions ranged over literature, journalism,
drama and the visual arts. A drama group was also started to put on
plays by Sayers, Williams, and Christopher Fry. James Brabazon,
Sayers's future biographer, first heard her talk there on the theater as the
kind of community the church should be and found his own vocation.
He said, however, that most of these illustrious Christians like Eliot did
not linger about the place once the job they had come for was done.

Eliot played a largely consulting role, often meeting with Father Mc-
Laughlin at Faber & Faber, but the winter of 1942-43 he and Philip
Mairet of the *New English Weekly* alternated chairing a discussion
group called "Towards the Definition of a Culture." Although they corresponded about St. Anne's affairs and exchanged news of mutual
friends, books, and so on, Eliot and Sayers never became close friends,
and she and Lewis joked a bit about Eliot's pontificating. But Sayers's
wartime poem, "Target Area" has an Eliot-like quality about the verse,
unlike her other more traditional poetry.

In 1944 Williams's second book of Arthurian poems, *The Region of the Summer Stars*, appeared. Williams was also busy with his last novel, *All Hallows' Eve*, which was completed in 1944 and published by Eliot's firm only three months before Williams died. It was not until 1945 that Williams actually carried out his threat to introduce Lewis to Eliot.

The three met for tea at the Mitre in Oxford, together with Father Gervase Mathew, whom Lewis's brother Warren had sarcastically called "the universal aunt" because of his fondness for pulling strings and arranging things. Mathew seems to have been the only witness who recounted the episode. He described both Lewis and Eliot as remarkably ill at ease, but his presence may not have helped, for later the two men became quite friendly.

On this occasion, Eliot began awkwardly by saying that Lewis was a much older man than he appeared in his photographs. He then told Lewis that he considered *Preface to Paradise Lost* to be Lewis's best book. Lewis apparently assumed that Eliot was deliberately bringing up his critical attack on Eliot's views of Milton, but he did not respond, so the conversation languished. According to Mathew, Williams enjoyed their embarrassment without trying to minimize it. It would take his death that May to bury the hatchet between them.

Before the Germans surrendered, Eliot wrote to American poet Allen Tate expressing a sense of pessimism about the postwar world. Just before V-E Day Eliot went to Paris, by then liberated, to repeat his 1943 lecture on "The Social Function of Poetry." In it he had expressed his hope that the intercommunication of Europe would continue without either separation or a unification that would lead to uniformity.

He returned from Paris to find that Charles Williams had suddenly died after surgery at Oxford. The first shock of the news hit Eliot just as the *Times* called to ask him to write Williams's obituary. In that paper Eliot wrote that Williams's death was a "very great personal loss and grief" to him and to literature and to England. But, as he wrote to Mrs. Williams on May 22, he could not grieve for Williams. His grief was for her and her son and the world. In the introduction to *Essays Presented to Charles Williams*, which Lewis, the other Inklings, and Sayers published with the help of Eliot, Lewis said that "the world seemed to us at that moment primarily a *strange* one." They all had a strong sense of Williams's abiding presence "everywhere" despite their great sense of loss. "When the idea of death and the idea of Williams met . . . it was the idea of death that was changed."

PART FOUR
Prophet 1945 – 1965

CHAPTER TEN

The Post-Christian World 1945-1955

*A*S ELIOT HAD FEARED, IN DEFEATING THE AXIS, THE UNITY OF European culture had been smashed. Eastern Europe was under Russian control and Western Europe was in desperate need of American aid. In England the Labour Party quickly won a resounding victory and tossed out Winston Churchill, who had relied on his rhetoric to preserve his government and the British empire. The Labour government then began implementing the ambitious Beveridge Plan for building Blake's "New Jerusalem," with which Eliot had already quarreled.

Initially the postwar national euphoria assumed that Labour could remake society by nationalizing industries, keeping the high war-time taxation, providing "cradle to grave" health insurance, and maintaining full employment. Regrettably, however, British industry was still not competitive. The balance of payments worked against the Labour program and the independence rapidly granted former colonies meant that Britain no longer had a privileged trading status. As Cold War tensions grew, Britain became torn between alliances with former colonies, who tended toward neutrality, or a growing alliance with America, with its Marshall Plan to rebuild Western Europe economically and with NATO for defense.

Life in England during the late '40s and early '50s remained grim and dour. For both victor and vanquished, food was poor and rationed; life was cold, gray, and regulated. Like C. S. Lewis and Dorothy L. Sayers, Eliot often wrote to thank his American fans, family, and friends for welcome food parcels.

Later Eliot admitted he had taken a great dislike to America's wartime president Franklin Roosevelt, who had just died in office. Eliot blamed FDR for his misguided diplomacy at Yalta, which benefited Russia and helped dismember the British empire, without creating a satisfactory substitute to prevent a return of the Dark Ages. By 1951 the Conservatives were in power again, but having only a slim majority, they did little to dismantle the welfare state.

Eliot expressed his criticism of FDR to the young American, William Turner Levy. After several missed opportunties, Levy finally met Eliot in 1948 in his Faber & Faber office where they shared some dreadful postwar tea. He then kept in touch with Eliot and saw him on Eliot's many trips to America. When Eliot first met Levy, he was an English graduate student at Columbia University. Levy became an English professor, but later was also ordained as an Anglican priest.

Their friendship grew out of Levy's enjoyment and understanding of Eliot's work and their shared religious beliefs. They also liked cats and *Pogo* cartoons, to which Levy introduced Eliot. Levy had the welcome quality of appreciating Eliot's company without trying to make something out of it; he took Eliot's slightly fussy, formal manner at face value, responded in a friendly fashion, and had the pleasure of watching Eliot become a family friend called Tom.

By now Eliot had moved back to London where he had agreed to share an apartment at 19 Carlyle Mansions, Cheyne Walk, in Chelsea, with the gregarious and caustic John Hayward. During the war Hayward had assumed more and more the role of friend and editor as well as custodian of the Eliot "image and archives."

Although there has been speculation about it, Eliot's motives for sharing Hayward's apartment seem to have been friendship and Christian charity. Hayward had become more and more crippled by multiple sclerosis, although he was still a social gadabout. He was also one of the most noted gossips in London, and he "dined out" often on Eliot stories.

Hayward said, for example, that he had wanted to "get Eliot away from all those parsons," a reference to Eliot's prewar life at St. Stephen's rectory. He also referred to Eliot as his "lodger." Many anecdotes are told about them at literary parties, where, typically, Eliot stood behind Hayward's wheelchair, saying little, but occasionally being coaxed by Hayward to perform. Eliot was also to be seen weekends pushing Hayward about Chelsea.

The two men shared a drawing room and dining room, furnished with Hayward's French antiques. They had a housekeeper and a cat named Pettipaws, whom Eliot told William Levy preferred to dine on rabbit. Hayward had a large bed-sitting room overlooking the Thames River. Eliot had a small study where he did his writing on a typewriter, standing up at a lectern desk, and a back bedroom in which he had only a bed, a crucifix, and a single light. Hayward made a great story out of the fact that Eliot had only a 60-watt bulb there, and, when pressed to spend some of the money he earned from *The Cocktail Party*, decided he might have a larger bulb. Hayward also kept his family and friends apart, so that his sister had never met Eliot until they were introduced to one another at a Buckingham Palace garden party.

Wherever he lived, Eliot followed his own routine. He went daily to Early Church at St. Stephen's, then came back to eat breakfast and write or work in his study until noon, when he left for Faber & Faber. There he dealt with their publishing in poetry and theology. He always attended the weekly "book committee day" with the other Faber directors, where Anne Ridler remembered his doing the *Times* crossword puzzle while contributing to the business discussion. She had become his secretary in 1938. She later married Vivian Ridler of the Oxford University Press and then left Faber & Faber during the war. She also noted Eliot's fondness for teasing people, or engaging in "oneupmanship."

At the office Eliot wrote standing up at his typewriter, and when dictating spoke in measured tones with perfectly formed sentences, much the way he normally talked. His deliberate manner, which offended or amused breezier souls, was also commented on by Levy who said that he once saw Eliot solemnly consult his watch with a gesture worthy of a far greater action. This manner was as characteristic of Eliot as Charles Williams's courtliness had been of him; both men appeared to belong to an older, more formal world.

Weekdays, Eliot lunched at one of his clubs, then worked until tea time, when he met with visitors or authors. He spent his evenings finishing work or studying, if Hayward did not persuade him to go to some party. He told Levy's mother that for recreation he liked to read detective stories and P. G. Wodehouse. He preferred Agatha Christie for her superb plots and guaranteed output of two books a year.

Throughout this period some observers described Eliot as lonely and withdrawn. But good friends like his American editor Robert Giroux remember that, although Eliot often played solitaire, when he had company he would push the cards aside and become his lively, amusing self. Eliot once told Auden that playing solitaire was the "nearest thing to being dead." Several critics took him literally, but, although his natural melancholy was real, the remark sounds like an Eliot joke. Giroux, Levy, Frank Morley, and others agreed that Eliot liked good company, food and drink, and told marvelous stories, often on himself, accompanied by his great booming laugh.

Increasingly, however, Eliot was to find it difficult to avoid being treated with embarrassing deference, while old acquaintances still complained that Eliot avoided them if he felt they were becoming too intimate. But most agreed that Eliot was, in the words of Stephen Spender, "considerate and sympathetic, in some very rare sense, a gentleman."

Together with his regular work and writing, Eliot continued to participate in St. Anne's House programs. On Ash Wednesday, 1946, for example, Eliot gave a talk on "Making Sense of the Universe" at Kingsway Hall, London. It was one of a Christian Mission series on "Religion and Philosophy" given during Lent by people like Dorothy L. Sayers and Monsignor Ronald Knox. On another occasion in 1951, Eliot gave the inaugural address for the St. Anne's drama series. It was called "The Social Significance of the Theatre."

Eliot was always loyal to friends in trouble (among whom he might well have classed his landlord Hayward with his debilitating disease). One of the best examples of this was his postwar efforts on behalf of his old friend and mentor Ezra Pound. During the '30s, Pound had become upset by the economic policies of the United States which he called "usury" (a Chestertonian "Distributist" term). Most people took Pound's ideas to be pure fascism, pro-Mussolini, and anti-Semitic, although they were really more anti-welfare statism than anything else.

When war broke out, Pound remained in Italy with his mistress Olga Rudge, a concert violinist, and their daughter Mary, to whom Pound taught Eliot's poem "The Hippopotamus." Like most English and American expatriates there, Pound was convinced that Mussolini had done well by Italy, but most of all Pound did not want a European war. Pound also believed there was an international (Jewish) conspiracy to make money out of war, and he wanted a strong Italy to counterbalance "Prussian" Germany in order to preserve Western civilization. Eliot shared Pound's concerns, if not his solutions.

Pound was asked by the Italians to broadcast to the United States on Rome Radio. He was allowed to speak freely, but he repeated his accusations that FDR was committing treason by helping international (Jewish) financiers wage war for their own gain. Pound's daughter Mary later felt that her father had "lost control of his own words" when he found he could not get his ideas across. Like the accusations made against P. G. Wodehouse, who broadcasted over German radio when interned in France, their comments were taken to be treason largely because they agreed to speak at all.

When the Americans took over Italy, partisans captured Pound and sold him to the Americans. Pound was indicted for treason and kept in a disgusting, open-air cage at Pisa. But, given a pencil and paper, Pound wrote his *Pisan Cantos*. The poems were published by Faber & Faber at Eliot's urging, and won the 1949 Bollingen Prize of the Library of Congress; Eliot was regarded as responsible for that award, although he was only one member of the distinguished committee.

When Pound was taken to Washington, D.C., to stand trial, Eliot cabled poet Archibald MacLeish, Assistant Secretary of State, saying he would do anything in his power to help Pound. He also wrote to other poets like Auden and Frost, asking for their public support and private testimony in case Pound was sentenced to death for treason. Pound, however, was declared mentally unfit to stand trial and was committed to St. Elizabeth's Hospital for the Criminally Insane.

On his first postwar trip to America in 1946 Eliot made a special effort to visit Pound (as he did on all subsequent trips). Each time, Eliot had to arrange to give a special lecture to cover his expenses because of the English government's strict restrictions on travel currency. It was eleven years before Pound was finally freed through the dogged efforts of Eliot and other friends.

Pound's daughter, Mary de Rachewiltz, went to London in 1949 en-route to America and visited Eliot in his Chelsea apartment. She described him as a tall, stooping man with a sad, enigmatic smile. Eliot entertained her in his study with its blocked-up fireplace, insisting on making their tea himself and giving her candy to take to her small son. Eliot told her he feared her father did not want to accept his freedom on the terms being offered and said it was a travesty that she should be sent to America to urge Pound to sign a statement that he was mad. In spite of her concern about her father, de Rachewiltz felt a strong urge to "mother" Eliot. She wanted to build him a roaring fire and fatten him up on bread and butter.

On his first visit to America in 1946 Eliot visited some of his poet protégés like W. H. Auden. Auden had spent the war in America and been greatly criticized for not returning to England to endure the war deprivations. But Eliot later commented that in terms of nationality, whatever Auden was, *he* was not, and vice versa. Whichever they were, Eliot and Auden had more in common now. Around 1940 Auden had returned to the Anglican Church in which he had been raised by his devout High Church mother. Auden's decision was greatly influenced by reading Charles Williams's *Descent of the Dove.*

Auden was now at work on "The Age of Anxiety." While some critics said that the poem showed more technical dexterity than personal development, Eliot commented that, on the contrary, Auden had let his spiritual development outstrip his technical ability.

In America, Eliot also visited his ailing brother and sisters and, as the youngest, now found himself obliged to assume more family responsibilities. He also saw Emily Hale again, as well as other family members like his cousin Eleanor Hinkley, who still lived in Cambridge and at whose house he met young Teddy Welch.

E. Martin Browne and Eliot had kept in touch throughout the war when Browne and his wife ran a traveling rep company. Then in October 1946 Browne successfully revived *The Family Reunion* at the

Mercury Theatre in London. After the experience of war and after *Four Quartets*, both critics and audiences understood the play far better and accepted it more enthusiastically. Browne then began to urge Eliot to write a new play.

Eliot kept saying that he had neither time nor energy for such a project. But during summer 1947 Rudolph Bing started the annual Edinburgh Festival, where Browne staged successful productions of both *Murder in the Cathedral* and *The Family Reunion*. Browne had to settle for doing a Christopher Fry play at Edinburgh the next year, but Eliot had finally begun to think about writing another play.

The year 1947, however, was a difficult one for Eliot. In January Vivien Eliot suddenly died. Vivien's brother Maurice had visited her not long before her death and concluded she was no more mad than he. John Hayward had the hard task of telling Eliot the news. Later Hayward gossipped to friends that Eliot reacted to this unexpected event with abnormal grief, which Hayward said showed that Eliot felt terrible remorse. But it would be surprising if Eliot had not felt grief, guilt, and pity for Vivien. That same year Eliot made a trip to America to see his brother, which meant writing and giving enough lectures to pay his way. Then his brother died, and he had to return again to help settle family affairs.

In these postwar lectures Eliot no longer acted like the stern young judge, but often reconsidered writers to whom he had previously been unsympathetic. Although he was not speaking directly about his beliefs, much of Eliot's later criticism also expressed his moral and religious concerns, as he tried to work out what led to religion or belonged with it or derived from it.

An example of his more benign approach to literature was his second talk on Milton, which he gave at the Frick Museum in New York. In it, like Lewis in *A Preface to Paradise Lost*, Eliot first paid homage to the late Charles Williams. He then moved his critical position on Milton closer to that of Williams (and Lewis). Instead of insisting on the divine right of poets to be the only critics, Eliot said he now thought that the scholar and the poet should work together at the task of criticism. Writers could not work in a state of continual revolution, so poetry should help prevent language from changing too fast. Finally, he stated that contemporary poets were far enough removed from Milton's time that they were in no danger of imitating him, and so could study him with profit.

Despite chronic ill health, increasingly aggravated by emphysema, Eliot continued his daily religious practices. He also went on retreats at places like Mirfield in Yorkshire. Later, in the middle '50s when his heart began to give him trouble, instead of going to Early Church at St. Stephen's, Eliot went to Chelsea Old Church on Cheyne Walk, the church long associated with Sir Thomas More. When possible, his friends the Fabers took him with them on winter trips. They went by ship to places like South Africa to get him out of England's difficult winter climate.

By contrast to 1947, 1948, his sixtieth year, was Eliot's "Annus Mirabilis." On January 1, 1948, the royal honors list was published, and Eliot had been awarded the Order of Merit. That award, the personal gift of the sovereign, was limited to twenty-four living men and women judged to be the most distinguished in their chosen work. His friends the Brownes held a small "homemade" celebration party, to which they invited only Bishop Bell of Chichester and a few other friends. Their invitation said "black tie." Eliot wrote back that he looked forward with great pleasure to this "very select party" and that his secretary had duly noted on his calendar that he must be sure to wear a black tie!

In March 1948 Eliot preached his first and only sermon in the chapel of Magdalene College, Cambridge. Eliot preached about his early, non-religious mentors like novelist George Eliot, and philosophers Herbert Spencer, Montaigne, and Bertrand Russell. He told the congregation that these writers had affected him in reverse, making a Christian out of him. Chesterton had testified to a similar paradoxical conversion progress in *Heretics* when he read G. B. Shaw and H. G. Wells, as did C. S. Lewis in *Surprised by Joy*.

Eliot ended his sermon by saying that he did not go to Early Church to set a good example for his housekeeper, because "influence by example" was only a byproduct of a Christian life. He added that most people never have to deal with a great betrayal or an earthshaking decision, but have to work to make penitence and humility the basis of their daily Christian life. Shortly afterward, Eliot was made an honorary Fellow of Magdalene College, where C. S. Lewis would soon take the college's new Chair of Medieval

Literature. Harvard had already awarded Eliot an honorary doctorate.

By June 1948 Eliot had a partial draft of the new play which he called "The One-Eyed Riley." He sent it to Browne, asking if he should continue with it, to which Browne simply replied "Yes." In September 1948 Eliot sailed for America again. He had been granted a visiting fellowship at Princeton's Institute for Advanced Study, where luminaries like Albert Einstein lived and thought undisturbed. Eliot had hoped to spend the winter peacefully finishing his new play, but he had been in America only a month when he was informed that he had been awarded the Nobel Prize for Literature. Since he had to go to Stockholm that December to receive it, he did not return to Princeton afterward. He told William Levy that the Nobel Prize particularly pleased him for poetry's sake but that it soon disrupted his privacy. Although his London literary friends felt he now outranked them, Eliot felt that the prize was a ticket to one's funeral because, as he told Geoffrey Faber, no one had ever written anything worthwhile after winning it.

On September 26, 1948, a *Festschrift*, or book of commemorative essays, was published in honor of Eliot's sixtieth birthday. *T. S. Eliot: A Symposium* was the first of three such volumes to appear, the last and best being edited as a memorial by poet-critic Allen Tate. This first one contained reminiscences by friends of Eliot's and accounts of other writers' reactions to his poetry. Among the contributors were his former secretary Anne Ridler; old friends like Conrad Aiken, Wyndham Lewis, Edith Sitwell, and Clive Bell; the younger generation of poets like W. H. Auden, Louis MacNeice, Stephen Spender, and John Betjeman; and friends like Brother George Every, Martin Browne, and Frank Morley.

In spite of, or perhaps because of, his increasing international fame, more and more critics accused Eliot of taking too casual an attitude toward his reputation. In their opinion he was being hypocritical; he must know that he was the premier living poet of the English language, if not of the world. Any self-deprecation on his part was said to be insincere, although no one has explained why arrogance would have been better. In part, of course, their criticism represented a dislike of his Christianity, which they suspected lay at the bottom of his unbecoming humility.

Eliot's *Notes towards the Definition of Culture* was published in England late in 1948. Parts had already been published in the *New English Weekly* during the war, and it was dedicated to the editor, his friend Philip Mairet. It represented Eliot's own thoughts based on discussions at The Moot and other Christian groups he had belonged to.

Notes towards the Definition of Culture was Eliot's last book-length effort to address directly the social and spiritual concerns he felt for Christendom in a post-Christian world. In it, as in *The Idea of a Christian Society* (later republished with it under the title *Christianity and Culture*), Eliot continued what he had begun in *After Strange Gods*. He was still seeking a cultural and ethical basis for a revitalized Christian society. He was not only speaking generally about the welfare state that was coming into being, but specifically assessing education's relationship to culture.

Unlike the more positive and argumentative approach of a Sayers or a Lewis, *Notes* was written in Eliot's famous tentative style. He posed questions and suggested answers, seeking to be descriptive, not dogmatic. His basic purpose was to define a word that he said was being tossed about again, the word *culture*. Like a doctrine that needs exact definition only after a heresy develops, Eliot suggested that since culture had now become a kind of synonym for "civilization" and was being used to support special views on education, the term itself must be carefully defined. In the constitution of UNESCO, for example, Eliot had found three different, contradictory definitions.

Eliot's main purpose in this book was to describe the "essential relationship" between culture and religion. To do so, he discussed the three social conditions needed for culture: organic (or class structure), geographic (or regional government), and a balance of unity and diversity in religion (he wanted a universality of doctrine combined with specific cultural devotion). Eliot did not want to write a prescription for culture, but to show what was needed for a (high) civilization. Finally, he hoped to "disentangle" culture from both politics and education. Clearly, he had set himself a huge agenda and could not cover it all, which was why he used the term "Notes."

Unlike those who claimed that their social, political, or educational changes would lead to a better culture or a "new" civilization, Eliot suggested that change may create a new civilization, but no one can predict what it will be like. New civilizations are born every day, but there is no standard for comparing one civilization with another.

He went on to suggest that culture is not a product that can be created deliberately; it is the result of different activities done for their own sakes. Therefore, each person should concentrate on his own work. It is the things we do individually that make the culture of an age different from other cultures.

Reversing Matthew Arnold, Eliot suggested that religion was not an element of culture but, on the contrary, culture was an element of religion. They were closely related because a people's culture could be called the "incarnation" of their religion. Culture could not be preserved or developed without religion, but religion also depended on culture. In terms of values, however, only "Christendom," as it should be, can be called the highest culture the world has ever known.

Eliot next tried to define the differences between a hereditary class based on family, in which remarkable individuals born outside it were added to it, and a state-supervised meritocracy. Eliot suspected that the meritocracy would become fragmented and would hold only mass values. But his real concern was the family, because the family was the means by which culture was passed on. Cultural life, he noted, grew out of the past, and it was the family that preserved the connections with tradition.

Eliot then discussed geographic regions and local roots. These regions were part of the organic whole that was Europe, but they allowed for a variety that kept culture alive without centralized planning and mass indoctrination. Social change ought to be restricted to particular problems, not reorganized from the center, because culture could not be "planned."

As Eliot saw it, Europe's different countries had gained from their interaction. He would not have drawn an "absolute line" between Europe and Asia, but he did recognize a European culture whose dominant aspect was the common tradition of Christianity. Europe's arts, laws, and thought were so rooted in Christianity that a European might not be a professing Christian, but everything he did came out of his Christian heritage. If this patrimony of culture were lost, all the state planning in the world would not bring Europe closer together.

Eliot was also concerned about the cultural importance of religious divisions, because they were closely related to the postwar interest in Christian unity. He liked the idea of a reunited Christendom, but not one that stood for the lowest credal denominator, compromising church integrity and episcopal authority. (It was for this reason that Eliot spoke out strongly against the postwar, interdenominational Church of South India, which Moot member Lesslie Newbigin helped to found.) At the same time, Eliot believed that any hope for world peace needed more than a world organization. It needed a common faith to unite it, together with endless conflict between ideas, because truth was defined by attacking false ideas or heresies.

Eliot next discussed the attempt of the modern state to use culture and education for its own purposes without being sure what either of them was. Impersonal forces and data led to the idea that culture could be planned, when culture really was the unconscious background of all planning. Eliot disagreed with contemporary assumptions that education could transmit culture, produce happiness, or train people. Education was the means of acquiring wisdom, knowledge, or learning, and more education for all only lowered the educational standard and encouraged the abandonment of the parts of culture that most needed transmission.

Because it was short, Eliot added to the end of the book a group of lectures he had given in Europe under official cultural auspices. He disliked such occasions because they did not allow much free interchange of ideas, but in one talk he made a fascinating plea for English as the most "European" of all languages because, as Dorothy L. Sayers had said, as a language English is a "mongrel" with the largest vocabulary in Europe. He ended by appealing to Europeans to preserve and transmit "our common culture." Europeans did not have to like one another or one another's work, but they must recognize their mutual dependence so that they could save part of the "goods" for which they were the trustees: Greece, Rome, Israel, and the legacy of Europe's past 2,000 years.

The book sold well because it came out just after Eliot had won the Order of Merit and the Nobel Prize, and it is still in print. But at the time and ever since, those critics who do not agree that the cultural basis of Western Civilization is Christianity complain that *Notes* is "astringent, dispassionate and prim," arguing a case instead of pleading a cause.

Eliot himself did not expect it to get much attention because the prevailing viewpoint was that orthodox Christian or nongovernmental solutions to human problems had been buried with the war. He would be interested to note how relevant his comments still sound in the late twentieth century. Since Eliot was returning to America often and had begun to write and speak more about his American roots, it should be noted that his idea of an "organic" society, to be perpetuated by a class that transmitted a regional "high culture" from generation to generation, was a good description of the Eliot family in America.

Eliot's internationalism, however, was being acted on to some extent in the political world. Within a few years of the publication of *Notes towards the Definition of Culture*, the Council of Europe was set up at Strasburg. In 1951 Eliot sent a letter of support to the conservative Union of Christian Democrats, whose British office was located at St. Anne's House. He told them he was not hoping to restore the Holy Roman Empire, but wanted to make modern Europeans more aware of the culture they still shared as a natural source of united purpose. His interest in the idea of a "unified" Europe lasted for the rest of his life, and as late as 1962 Eliot spoke out publicly in favor of England's entering the Common Market.

Years before, when Eliot was a bright new star in the London literary heavens, Wyndham Lewis had painted his portrait as an angular, apprehensive young man in a three-piece suit. Now in 1949 Wyndham Lewis painted his second portrait of Eliot. In a *Time* interview Lewis said he wanted to show Eliot as someone "who expected the worst," but, in contrast to his earlier portrait, Lewis's later work simply showed Eliot as older and tired.

Although Eliot did what was expected of him, he was frustrated in finishing his new play by the amount of time stolen by public occasions. To add to his sense of pressure, Eliot also knew that any major work he produced after winning the Nobel Prize must be special. He need not have worried. His play, whose title became *The Cocktail Party*, was to be Eliot's greatest commercial success, introducing his work to a far wider audience than he had reached before.

In *The Cocktail Party* Eliot expressed in dramatic form many of his ideas about the "Terrestial City" (the here and now). Community was now central to Eliot's thought, so he showed saints only in relationship to the City. *The Cocktail Party* is probably the best example in Eliot's work of Charles Williams's idea of the co-inhered society. While Eliot still explored both spiritual Ways of Affirmation and Negation because both were equally valid, Eliot's cast in this play was no longer divided into sheep and goats—or the damned and the blessed. His final message was simply that in the end there is only one choice, choosing or not choosing to be yourself.

Writing a drawing-room comedy aimed at the West End represented a definite choice on his part, just as going from medieval drama to modern had been. But as Dorothy L. Sayers expressed it in "Playwrights are not Evangelists," professional playwrights like herself and Eliot could not and should not write plays just to "do good." If their artistic imagination had been kindled like Dante's by a spiritual illumination, to write about that experience was entirely appropriate. But if they were asked (as they both were) to follow up a successful play on St. Athanasius with one on St. Augustine, without any creative impulse to do so, they would be writing "outside the range of their spiritual experience" and would do bad work. Instead, she urged the church to let playwrights choose their own plays, but then support them by attending them, talking about them, and including them within the wider Christian culture.

By writing drawing room comedies, Eliot hoped not only to reach a larger audience, but he was taking a stand against the temper of the times, which still saw the human condition as tragic and fragmented. Dramatically, comic man, unlike tragic man who sees life as a prison, takes life as it comes. Eliot was suggesting that it was possible to redeem the time, as well as show human beings as imperfect and earthbound. Instead of portraying a universal, almost Gnostic sensibility, like a work by Virginia Woolf, Eliot involved himself and his audience in ordinary experiences common to mankind.

Comic characters by definition can achieve joy, but only after they have journeyed through the real world and have their faith in its permanence restored. A comic character needs to slip on a banana peel, then, after picking himself up, realize that he has survived the attack on his pride. The catharsis of comedy comes from recognizing that the trials and tribulations of everyday life can be paths toward what is ultimately significant.

Therefore, in his usual indirect way, Eliot was preaching the gospel. In the Gifford Lectures, Archbishop William Temple had declared that Christianity was the most materialistic of all religions. Both the Creation and the Incarnation had made a profound respect for ordinary existence a part of faith, so that comedy and Christianity belonged together. Eliot's wish to write Christian comedies was based not only on his wish to reach a larger audience and be socially relevant, but also to represent his personal faith as it had been expressed in *Four Quartets*. In that poem Eliot had moved from his sense of tragic isolation toward acceptance of ordinary life in the world. As a result, many critics have called his last three plays "footnotes" to *Four Quartets*, as well as a dramatization of Eliot's ideas on society found in *The Idea of a Christian Society* and *Notes towards the Definition of Culture*.

In a talk given by Dorothy Sayers at St. Anne's House in 1951, she defined the types of Christian drama with specific references to Eliot's plays. According to her, the traditional types were the mystery play, which told the Christian Myth; the miracle play, with sacred or supernatural characters, in which category Sayers included *Murder in the Cathedral*; and the morality play, like *Everyman* and *The Cocktail Party*. Sayers said that *The Family Reunion* with its Furies was a borderline miracle-morality play, as well as a borderline Christian tragedy. The true morality play was the forerunner of the modern psychological drama because it dealt with problems of human conduct in terms of Christian faith and morals. Charges of obscurity brought against modern morality plays like *The Cocktail Party*, she said, came from the general public's ignorance of the Christian story.

As a genre, comedy (or morality plays) has always been didactic and makes use of fantastic plots without deep characterizations. In his plays, therefore, Eliot did not try to create dramatic, psychological novels, but made use of artificial surprise and coincidences and different types of people to express certain truths about man as a social being.

Like his other major works, *The Cocktail Party* was written in close collaboration with others. As Eliot acknowledged in the dedication, John Hayward had helped with the many revisions of the text, but

Eliot's main editor was still Martin Browne, who also produced the finished play. Once again Browne cut, sharpened, and refined Eliot's play to make it work onstage.

Eliot suggested afterward that writing *Four Quartets* had taught him to simplify his language, while experience and maturity had made him abler to say what he wanted. In *The Cocktail Party*, he deliberately did not use poetic language because he felt that in *The Family Reunion* the poetry had gotten in the way of the plot. He told a Chicago audience in 1959 that he could read aloud from only two of his plays, *Murder* and *The Family Reunion*, because the others had no passages complete in themselves. But Eliot's early drafts still indulged "in argument, hypothesis, and generalized philosophic reflection," and Browne had to help Eliot eliminate this indirectness and let characters speak directly to one another.

The Cocktail Party takes place within C. S. Lewis's "bent world," which is recognizably the "Waste Land" of the Hollow Men. It is the story of an unhappy marriage which is "saved" in a manner reminiscent of the marriage of Mark and Jane in *That Hideous Strength*. Both works were based on the convention of modern social comedy that the most important thing for men and women was the fulfillment of their personalities in love.

In Eliot's play both partners have had an affair with another person, and these four make up the "quartet" of main characters. Its plot and its witty, brittle conversation are intentionally like other drawing-room comedies of the period, from Somerset Maugham's prewar *The Constant Wife* to Noel Coward's postwar *Quadrille*. Like other Eliot plays, *The Cocktail Party*'s plot also had its roots in Greek drama. Eliot used the myth about King Admetus, whose wife Alcestis agreed to die in his place to pacify the god Apollo. Alcestis was restored to life when Hercules intervened, making Eliot wonder what happened when Alcestis came back.

His play opens with a husband whose wife has just left him, so that he is faced with a cocktail party which he is too proud to cancel. But he tells a stranger what has really happened, and the stranger offers to bring her back. He does so, then helps the couple recognize that their real natures, when accepted, make them admirably suited to one another after all.

Against the background of this mundane modern couple's marriage, the husband's mistress Celia discovers that her true destiny is not love affairs but sainthood. But her martyrdom is not the real center of the play. The true center is the unnamed Power who works within the heart or conscience of everyone. Eliot's title stands for modern society's superficial community, which is only a prelude to the banquet of life.

Eliot introduced an element of fantasy with his two busybody Guardians (angels) who are guests at the party, as well as Sir Henry Harcourt-Reilly, the stranger who turns out to be a psychiatrist with insights into the other characters. By using these "supernatural" characters, Eliot combined in this play the themes of *The Family Reunion* and *Murder in the Cathedral*, producing a mystifying whole, whose plot depends on a kind of "Christian conspiracy." Charles Williams's influence was very noticeable in the Guardians, and Eliot also quoted Shelley about "the Magus Zoroaster . . . who met his own image walking in the garden."

As producer, Martin Browne found that the most difficult thing in the play was Celia's offstage death as a martyr. The announcement changed the mood of the play abruptly in the third act, but Browne still felt that it "worked." He first persuaded Eliot to be more graphic about what happened to Celia, but then had to persuade Eliot to tone it down a bit. Eliot had not only crucified Celia on an ant hill, but smeared her with juice to attract the ants. The ant hill is an Eliot image of the "unreal city" of *The Waste Land*, filled with teeming unredeemed men and women; it is also an image of the hill outside Jerusalem, where Christ was crucified. Her death was too graphic for some audiences, while critics felt it made the rest of the last act an anticlimax.

Some felt that having his spiritual guide be a psychiatrist was a stumbling block, because the role is too close to modern secular faith. But Eliot had deliberately chosen such a person to try to bridge the gap between Christian belief and the modern understanding. The Chamberlaynes's future life does not have many "moments of vision" and in spite of their admission of sin and the revelation of divine grace in ordinary life, their world remained too close to the banal and empty world of Prufrock. Much of this impression depends on how Act III is played; in a recent London production where Lavinia came onstage pregnant, the

Chamberlaynes' life seemed likely to be lived realistically and humorously "happily ever after."

During the writing of the play, Browne had been negotiating to perform it at the Edinburgh Festival, then take it to a London theater. When Festival director Bing announced that Browne might not be allowed to produce the play at Edinburgh, Eliot said that either Browne produced the play or it would not be done. It finally was produced by Browne and the West End's Henry Sherek, beginning a three-way collaboration between Eliot, Sherek, and Browne that lasted amicably until Eliot's death.

The opening cast in Edinburgh had both Cathleen Nesbitt and Irene Worth, and the play made Alec Guinness, who played the psychiatrist, a star. It opened at the Lyceum on Monday, August 22, 1949, and was a smash hit, but played in Edinburgh only during the week of the festival. No London theater was available, so, after a brief Christmas run at Brighton's Theatre Royale, Sherek took it to New York where it opened on January 21, 1950, again a huge success.

The Cocktail Party sold over 50,000 copies in print and was probably the most thoroughly criticized play of its time, though audiences still tended to ask "What does it mean?" Most reviews were favorable—several used the word *masterpiece*—but those "against" the play said that it had too many religious overtones, or was not dramatic enough or poetic enough. Others simply asserted that by comparison with his poetry Eliot's plays were too labored, precious, and aesthetically disappointing.

Seen and heard, however, his plays are remarkably effective and very "speakable," ranging from chatter and gossip to serious self-probing without losing rhythmic vitality. They imposed a credible order on ordinary reality and kept a Christian presence onstage in the "post-Christian" world.

The Cocktail Party finally returned to London, where it was already a legend, and ran for over one hundred performances in the West End. All told, it grossed over a million dollars. Eliot's profit was about 29,000 pounds, of which punitive English taxation took 25,000. But together with his Nobel Prize money (11,000 pounds), his Faber & Faber salary of about 4,000 pounds, and about 2,500 pounds a year in royalties, Eliot was now rich for a poet. He still had to pay his own way in America because he could take very little English money out of the country.

During August 1949 Eliot was once again in need of a secretary. He interviewed several and hired a young woman named Esme Valerie Fletcher who came from Yorkshire. Miss Fletcher had been fascinated by Eliot's poetry since her school days when she first heard "Journey of the Magi." Her ambition had been to be the private secretary of a famous writer, and after finishing school she had accomplished it by coming to London to work for novelist and playwright Charles Morgan.

Then she heard about the Eliot position through a family friend and applied for it. During her interview, Eliot smoked the entire time, acting as nervous as she felt, and never looked at her, but at the floor. She later told Eliot's American relatives, the Welches, that she had quickly realized that Eliot was very shy and dreadfully nervous about interviewing people. Much to his relief, she quickwittedly began to interview herself and got the job.

Valerie Fletcher remained as Eliot's efficient secretary for the next seven years. She was highly competent and cheerful, and during his repeated illnesses gradually took charge of more and more of his affairs. But she continued to call him "Mr. Eliot" and to behave so formally that it took Eliot seven years to realize that, like any number of other women both American and British, she was in love with him.

A private printing of Eliot's *Poems Written in Early Youth* came out in 1950 and was later reissued by Faber & Faber. With the Fabers Eliot again went to South Africa to avoid the English winter fogs. On March 6, 1950, he was featured on the cover of *Time* magazine as its man of the moment. Eliot was now a genuine celebrity whom people came to see or hear just because he was there; he and his work had become a household word. He was pawed and surrounded on public occasions, and had to keep his address and phone number private to avoid fans. But until his second marriage, when he finally had someone else with whom to share the rewards of fame, Eliot wrote William Levy that he found most of this public adulation uncomfortable and embarrassing.

Although he was reasonably affluent, Eliot was still precise and methodical about his expenses and tended to be a bit tight. Yet he secretly helped a number of writers from Dylan Thomas to Wyndham Lewis, and he liked giving presents to his friends. Levy casually asked him for a crucifix, assuming that Eliot had several. On his next visit Eliot brought him a handsome silver crucifix made specially by Dunstan Pruden, a pupil of the famous sculptor Eric Gill.

In his turn, Levy delighted in finding special things to give to Eliot. These gifts included a piece of Lincoln memorabilia, which reminded Eliot of a Lincoln portrait that had hung in his St. Louis home, as well as any number of stray books, which had once belonged to Eliot but, lost, had found their way into the public market.

In November 1950 Eliot gave four lectures on "The Aims of Education" at the University of Chicago. They were later published in the posthumous collection, To Criticize the Critic. In them Eliot again criticized the contemporary idea of achieving efficiency and equality in education, or seeking to use "social engineering" on problems of human existence. He was far more concerned with improving the quality of existing education than extending the length of time a student was in school. But, most of all, Eliot declared that education must transcend the purposes of any particular political system because its goals must include teaching students to earn a living, to enjoy life, and to be good citizens.

Eliot saw the greatest danger to education to be the increasing influence of the state, so that with all its faults he felt that democracy was still the best form of society. It might give room to good and bad men alike, but in democracy there was no total rule. There, scientists, scholars, and artists could rule in their own domains without being called deviationist, defeatist, or decadent.

Many Chicagoans, not just students and faculty, had lined up to see and hear the great man speak. At a university reception Eliot asked Chancellor Robert Hutchins why he had written that Eliot was more of a democrat than Edmund Burke. In spite of the lectures Eliot had just given, which showed that he was not a reactionary "royalist" at all times and in all places, Eliot told Hutchins that he thought Burke was the greater democrat. Characteristically, Hutchins walked away without replying. Eliot remained at Chicago as poet in residence for what he told Levy was a "wonderful but very exhausting" month. That year Eliot also gave the first Theodore Spencer Memorial Lecture at Harvard, in which he discussed his current interest in poetry and drama.

His friend William Levy was now at Union Theological Seminary, studying for the Episcopal priesthood. While there, Levy became acquainted with theologian Reinhold Niebuhr, an old friend of Eliot's from The Moot, and he arranged for Eliot to meet Niebuhr again in New York. Eliot then arranged for Faber & Faber to take over publishing Niebuhr's work in England.

Back in America once more in 1952, Eliot went to church with Levy and his parents, but the service was a disaster. The organ quit, so the choir had to sing a cappella, then the organ began to screech during the sermon, which turned out to be a report on the parish fair. When Levy introduced Eliot to the rector's wife, she introduced her three children to "Mr. C. S. Lewis." Amused, Eliot told the rector that as church warden, he was used to minor disruptions of all kinds in church. After church Levy took Eliot to see the New York Zoo, where they visited Eliot's favorite animals, the 'possums and hippopotami, and talked about church congregations and outreach.

In the midst of fulfilling the time-consuming role of being a living literary legend and being treated as oracle as well as poet, Eliot was writing another play. He had begun it as early as 1950, working on it with John Hayward, but it was not until 1952 that Martin Browne saw a complete draft of *The Confidential Clerk*.

This play was loosely based on the Greek comedy *Ion*, but Eliot had doubled the abandoned boys and added an illegitimate daughter. He used the plot's fantastic mixups to explore the problem of personal identity, again asking Prufrock's overwhelming question, "Who am I?" This play was also about choices, but its choices were made long ago, and now they must be accepted and lived with.

Browne described the resulting play as written in the style of "W. S. Gilbert mixed with Oscar Wilde," with a suburban Pallas Athene to clear up the tangles. Unlike *The Cocktail Party*, *The Confidential Clerk* ended with a strong third act and a superb final curtain.

The characters' names recall the younger Eliot's fondness for odd names like Skimbleshanks or Prufrock. The hero who is seeking his true father and vocation was originally called Ian Sympkins, then became Slingsby, and ended up Colby Simpkins. His supposed half-sister is Lucasta Angel, while her fiance is B. (for Barnabas) Kaghan.

Browne spent many days working with Eliot in his little study in Chelsea, trying to keep the characters "alive" throughout the play, with its multiple identities and mixed-up comings and goings. Eliot's poetic sense appeared only in the structure and characters; there were very few times when the audience heard Eliot the "maker of immortal phrases." The only poetic scene is the one in which Colby and Lucasta talk about themselves, using the familiar Eliot imagery of doorways and gardens.

The Confidential Clerk does employ common Eliot themes: the interrelatedness of our lives, the need to make decisions and accept their consequences, the importance of finding one's true vocation, the seriousness of self-deception, and the danger of trying to run other people's lives.

Some of its characters resemble earlier Eliot characters. Eggerson, the confidential clerk, whom Eliot said was "the only developed Christian in the play," is a spiritual guide something like the psychiatrist in *The Cocktail Party*. Like that play's married couple, the Chamberlaynes, Sir Claude and Lady Elizabeth, must also settle for what they have—two unexpected children, instead of the hero, Colby Simpkins, who is the son everyone wants.

Eliot's characters are seeking to trace their identity (or inheritance). Some, especially Colby Simpkins, are working at resolving the familiar Eliot "two Ways" dilemma. But most of them are seeking relationships with other people in the City. Only Colby discovers that he wants to be free of other people to follow his true vocation. Although the clerk, Eggerson, suggests that Colby may end up ordained, as a "saint" Colby is considerably less removed from society than Harry in *The Family Reunion* or Celia in *The Cocktail Party*.

In 1953 when Eliot next saw Father Levy, now ordained, in New York, they talked about *The Confidential Clerk*. Eliot told Levy he always came to rehearsals prepared to cut or rewrite because playwriting was not something completed in a study but a "communal enterprise." Eliot also told Levy that audiences would find *The Confidential Clerk* less profound than *The Cocktail Party* but really it was more so.

The play was presented at the 1953 Edinburgh Festival with a stellar cast and was highly successful. Audiences enjoyed it, but many left wondering what the message was under its farcical surface. Reviewers said that the audience did not need to worry about the play's being written in verse because they would never notice. They added that the play was Eliot's best technically, achieving a unity he had never had before.

One critic declared that the play was rudimentary, but no one dared to say so because it was a classic case of the emperor's new clothes. The comment was also made that it was a Victorian melodrama unsuited to the modern world. By putting a cliché-uttering clerk at the play's center, with a spiritually elect "fool" (Colby) as his foil, Eliot put his actors under a lot of stress. Having made it plain that "the poetry did not matter," critics felt that Eliot had considerably weakened his dramatic effect. Others have called *The Confidential Clerk* a tour de force, created as self-conscious theater and manipulated for Eliot's own purposes.

But, as Dame Helen Gardner suggested in her 1965 lecture on the comedies of T. S. Eliot, the tradition of social comedy is a very tough tradition. It has broken out again and again for the past two thousand years. To catch the tone of an age is the merit of high comedy, and these plays do catch the accents of "polite society" in the postwar world. At the same time, in these plays, Eliot "embodied" the problems and solutions he had also discussed in his important social criticism. Finally, Gardiner added that her own earliest introduction to the Christian faith had not been through great art or an impressive intellectual system of thought, but in the grace of many obscurely faithful lives like that of Eliot's confidential clerk.

When he came to America, Eliot especially enjoyed visiting the Levys in their New York apartment above the Hudson because it reminded him of the Thames and the Mississippi. On his 1953 trip, Eliot returned to St. Louis, where he spoke at Washington University about the American language and literature. In this lecture Eliot talked at length about his memories and his American roots. But back in New York, Eliot told Father Levy that he must come to England, where Eliot would take him to visit an English abbey, where he often stayed and where he now planned to end his days.

CHAPTER ELEVEN

Elder Statesman 1955 – 1965

*T*S. ELIOT'S LAST YEARS WERE MARKED BY ENGLAND'S INCREASING prosperity under a Conservative government. By 1955 Winston Churchill had retired, leaving Anthony Eden (a former Moot member whom Eliot admired) as his successor. Under Eden's leadership both Italy and West Germany were admitted to NATO in defense of Western Europe. In the old empire, decolonization continued, but the situation in the Middle East remained tensely divided between Arabs and Israelis.

The Labour Party had lost out because it could not reconcile social planning with democracy. Eliot wrote American conservative Russell Kirk that it also was interesting to see a genuine conservativism start in America, where liberalism had flourished for so long. But he thought William Buckley's *National Review* too consciously represented a "defiant" minority. Eliot saw American politics in general as too full of personalities and not full enough of principles.

In 1955 Eliot made his last major statement on political thought;

during his remaining years he never completed his planned review and publication of his social criticism. This talk, called "The Literature of Politics," was given at a luncheon sponsored by the London Conservative Union and was published after his death in *To Criticize the Critic*.

In the speech, Eliot wittily declined to count himself a political philosopher, even though "interchange" between politics and literature often occurred in his work. Eliot began by seeking to show that truth often lies between two extremes. He described two lines of development common to politics: one, a doctrinaire, ideological party that has to learn in office that theory and circumstance often collide; the other, a pragmatic party that ends by abandoning principle altogether. Each had its dangers, but he felt that the latter was more organic in the Burkian Conservative sense.

Then he spoke out against historical determinism, another name for progress, which appealed to those who believe in the unlimited possibilities of planning or those who like to feel they are moving with the tide. Eliot felt that private experience teaches us that every reform leads to new abuses. He was glad he did not have to avoid being either a fanatic or an opportunist the way politicians did.

As for the influence of writers on the political process, he thought that a writer should work in the area of "pre-politics," seeking to penetrate to the core of a problem. The writer should try to arrive at the truth and set it forth, but without much hope of changing the present course of events. Among those he saw doing this work were his old acquaintances from The Moot, Reinhold Niebuhr and Christopher Dawson. Finally, echoing The Moot's main thrust, Eliot wanted men of action and men of thought to know and talk to one another. Ultimately, however, all political thinking enters the domain of ethics, which is really the domain of theology. It then must be judged by what it answers to the questions: What is Man? What are his limitations, misery, greatness, and finally, his destiny? In a BBC talk a year later, Eliot said he felt that the present alternative to a Christian culture was no longer a pagan society, but one without any religion or culture at all. Eliot was once more to suggest answers to those fundamental questions in his last play, *The Elder Statesman*.

As Russell Kirk testifies, Eliot by now had achieved a genial serenity which made him very good company. By accepting life on its own terms, as Sir Claude learned to do in *The Confidential Clerk*, Eliot was neither puffed up by success nor reacting to old age with the anger and despair of Shaw, Wells, Pound, or Wyndham Lewis. Eliot felt that if the present age made an end of its own culture, that was in the hands of God. Unlike Malcolm Muggeridge, who was to move from being a socialist to being a believer, while still maintaining his dialectical view of history, Eliot never regarded "the end of Christendom" as a consummation devoutly to be wished.

Increasingly frail, and in and out of the hospital, Eliot gave precious time to helping friends who needed it, from his crippled landlord John Hayward, to his old friends Wyndham Lewis and Ezra Pound. By 1954 his recurring bronchitis, which in turn aggravated his irregular heartbeat problems, obliged Eliot to give up cigarettes. As a result he broke the Puritan training of a lifetime and guiltily began to nibble candy.

He continued to visit the United States once a year, but when he won the Hanseatic Goethe Prize in 1954, it was 1955 before he was well enough to fly to Hamburg to receive it. There Eliot gave a talk on Goethe the Sage. His description of the benign, elderly Goethe, still alert and filled with the wisdom of age, might be mistaken for a portrait of Eliot himself, seen as a latter-day Great European.

Eliot continued to work at Faber & Faber where he played the role of very senior "confidential clerk," although he made the publishing mistake of advising against George Orwell's *Animal Farm*. One of his last poems, "The Cultivation of Christmas Trees," was published as a Faber *Ariel Poem* in 1954, and Eliot sent it as a Christmas card to friends like Father Levy and Russell Kirk.

By January 1956 Eliot had managed to write two acts of his last play, tentatively called "The Rest Cure," which was to become *The Elder Statesman*. That April he returned to America where he gave a lecture on April 30 to nearly 14,000 people in a baseball stadium at the University of Minnesota. It was the largest group ever assembled to hear anyone discuss literature; Eliot told Levy it made him feel like a very small bull in a very large arena.

His topic was the frontiers of criticism, by which he meant the point beyond which criticism becomes something else, like psychology or biography. Eliot felt that modern literary criticism had developed from the work of Coleridge, who had first shown the relevance of other disciplines like philosophy, aesthetics, and psychology to literary studies. But, in the last analysis, for Eliot the critic's task was not to explain literature or the writer, but to help the reader understand and enjoy the poetry.

Eliot told his vast Minnesota audience that he had written criticism only on books or writers that had come his way; he had not set out deliberately to create a body of critical work. Now he was worried that academic criticism was becoming pedantic and unrelated to the act of creation. He cheerfully confessed that his Notes to *The Waste Land* were a gigantic waste of time. Too much seeking after sources confused knowledge with the "newness," which was what creation was all about. Eliot did not object to biographies of poets, but he warned his vast audience not to rely too much on psychological or biographical guesswork which could destroy their direct experience of the work.

During 1956 one of his sisters died, and Eliot himself was ill again. But he wrote to an old friend that he was far more upset by public events like the Soviet's brutal invasion of Hungary. Next, when Egypt's Nasser defiantly nationalized the Suez Canal, the English and French, with Israeli support, attacked Egypt. They found themselves labeled aggressors in the United Nations and abandoned diplomatically by the United States.

The Suez crisis did not drive the Conservative Party from office, but by the end of the year Prime Minister Anthony Eden had retired. His successor was publisher Harold Macmillan, who presided over an increasingly "liberated" and "affluent society" that lasted for what remained of Eliot's life. The costly welfare state paradoxically continued, too, administered by a civil service still dominated by "Old School Ties."

Near the end of 1956, in their office at Faber & Faber, Eliot suddenly proposed to his secretary, Valerie Fletcher. After she accepted his proposal, Eliot told her she had maintained such a businesslike front, even when they had visited mutual friends, that he was not positive she even liked him. Their marriage was a huge success, and their delight in one another made most of their friends extremely happy. Mrs. Eliot later commented in a newspaper interview that Eliot had needed a happy marriage because "there was a little boy in him that had never been released." Eliot said he had not been so happy since childhood.

Since Eliot was sixty-eight and world famous, and she was thirty and had been his secretary, their marriage inevitably led to gossip. Although his future bride was afraid that the thought of gossip might make Eliot change his mind, once he had decided to act, Eliot did so. He arranged for them to be married in secret without publishing the banns to alert the press, very much the way he had arranged for his private baptism and confirmation.

They were married on January 10, 1957, at 6:15 in the morning at St. Barnabas Church, with only her parents and his solicitor, who was the best man, present. Later they found out that Eliot's youthful poetic model, Jules Laforgue, had been married at St. Barnabas too.

The only real loser by Eliot's marriage was his friend John Hayward, who had come to rely on him. Hayward was upset by the marriage, and gossiped about the new couple, causing an estrangement between them. Several other Eliot friends like Emily Hale were also upset or disappointed.

After a honeymoon and a stay in hotels, the couple moved that April into an apartment in Kensington Court Gardens. It was located just off Kensington High Street, and also near the flat in Cornwall Gardens where Eliot had lived long ago. Recently, one of the blue London English heritage plaques that mark famous authors' residences was placed in Kensington Court Gardens. The present poet laureate, Ted Hughes, an Eliot protege, delivered a short oration. Hughes was joined at the ceremony by poet Sir Stephen Spender, another Eliot protege who wrote a biography of him, and by actor Sir Alec Guinness. Much of the current tourist interest in Eliot is the result of *CATS!*, the fantastic musical based on Eliot's poems about his Kensington pets like Mungojerrie and Rumpelteazer.

The year before, C. S. Lewis had married American Joy Davidman in a civil ceremony to give her and her sons British citizenship. She then was diagnosed as having cancer, and within two months of the Eliots' marriage, Lewis had married Joy in a religious ceremony at the hospital. Lewis was now a professor at Cambridge, having finally accepted the new chair at Magdalene College, which had been offered to Helen Gardner, the Eliot expert, when Lewis first refused it.

There are interesting parallels between Eliot's and Lewis's marriages, coming near the end of their lives. Suddenly made happy, both men expressed the same kind of awestruck wonder at the sudden change in the emotional climate of their lives; both were oblivious of unkind and silly comment. Both wives were bright, intelligent Christian women, who were greatly interested in their husband's work, although Valerie Eliot admitted that she always tried hard to get out of giving criticism when asked. Although ill health soon ended both marriages, the two couples also became acquainted. Their meeting occurred after Lewis and Eliot began to work together on the Commission for the Revision of the Psalter, which finally ended the literary feud between them.

On Poetry and Poets, a collection of Eliot's essays, was published in 1957. Although he did not change any of the texts themselves, both by his selection and his introduction, Eliot subtly indicated his final judgment on his own and others' poetry. He was to perform the same kind of evaluation of his own literary criticism in his convocation lecture at Leeds in 1961 where he finally admitted that he did belong in the august line of English poet-critics like Dryden, Johnson, Coleridge, and Matthew Arnold.

By the end of 1957 Eliot had completed his last play, but he wrote Father Levy that his marriage had made it a very different work from what he had planned originally. His collaborator Martin Browne, for example, while rejoicing in Eliot's marriage, found that Eliot's wish to add "love interest" meant a great deal of rewriting. Browne was also annoyed because the press discovered that the "Happy Eliots" made good copy, and reporters began to haunt rehearsals.

Like many other critics, Browne's final judgment was that *The Elder Statesman* is a weak play. The main complaints made against it are that it deals only with private lives and lacks dramatic action. The best description of the play, however, is Helen Gardner's comment that it is an unfinished picture from a master's hand, with only some parts worked up, like a Leonardo or Michelangelo "cartoon."

The play was based on Sophocles' *Oedipus at Colonus*, but it does not have quite enough of Eliot's inventive, comic twists to make a strong plot. In some ways, too, *The Elder Statesman* is not really a comedy. Despite its witty scenes and happy ending, it is closer to Dorothy L. Sayers's borderline category between a miracle play and a morality play, having some unmistakable echoes from both *Murder in the Cathedral* and *The Family Reunion*.

The main character is Lord Claverton, a former statesman who, accompanied by his daughter Monica, goes to a fancy nursing home to die. Here, at death's door, two people from Lord Claverton's past appear and accuse him of ruining them. To face them, Lord Claverton must also face himself as he really is. He is brought to see that his life has been a fraud, an escape from himself, and a projection of the person he wanted others to see. He is, in fact, one of Eliot's "Hollow Men."

The grim jest is that these two ghosts, a wealthy ex-chorus girl and a fellow student and felon turned millionaire, were not really ruined by his actions. But without his desertion they might have become better people. Like the tempters in *Murder in the Cathedral*, these persons really represent the times in Lord Claverton's life when he was afraid to let the world see him as he really was—and therefore made cowardly retreats. Lord Claverton finally admits the truth about himself to himself and to his daughter Monica. Since she is the one person he really cares about, when her father confesses his sins to her and finds that she does not stop loving him, he is free to die in peace.

For those who do not find *The Elder Statesman* merely an old man's "folly," the play is another dramatization of Eliot's theme of a "turning," or the story of *Everyman* told in modern dress. For all his former status, Lord Claverton is not one of the elect, chosen for a special spiritual destiny, nor does he expiate any sins other than his own. But like his creator, he achieves the serenity with which the play is filled, suggesting (as Eliot wrote in the play's dedication to his wife) that it is only by living in community that the limitations of human understanding are overcome by love.

By confessing his youthful sins to his daughter, Lord Claverton finally dares to be an "explorer." *The Elder Statesman* is closely related not only to Eliot's poems about the unhappy statesman, "Coriolan," but to the somber passage in "Little Gidding" on the "gifts reserved for age," where Eliot spoke of the rending pain of reenacting all you have done and been.

There is general agreement that Eliot's love scenes, though sincere, verge on the mawkish, but the play's dialogue still shows Eliot's marvelous grasp of the "heightened speech" he had created for comedy.

There is also a slight increase in the actual "poetry" which he allowed himself to use as the play moved toward its end, suggesting that future plays might have had still more.

In December 1957 Dorothy L. Sayers died suddenly, leaving her translation of Dante to be completed by her friend Barbara Reynolds. In her first book of essays on Dante, published in 1954, Sayers had mentioned with approval Eliot's discussion of metaphor in Dante and had also quoted from *The Cocktail Party* to describe the difference between the way of a great saint and an ordinary person. Now, it seemed, the role of Christian spokesman for literature was left to Eliot and C. S. Lewis.

Lewis, who wrote the panegyric read by Bishop Bell at Sayers's memorial service, was at work on *Reflections on the Psalms*, which was published the following year. Its publication resulted in Lewis's being asked to serve with Eliot on a committee of seven which had been appointed to revise (not retranslate) *The Psalter* of *The Book of Common Prayer*. This select body was appointed by the Convocations of Canterbury and York. Their committee met from 1959 through 1962, and the results were published in 1963 as *The Revised Psalter*. Eliot told Levy that the commission worked very hard to find the right word to make plain the sense and not destroy the work itself, while Lewis was much amused when it was pointed out that their efforts were like Kipling's story "Proofs of Holy Writ," in which Ben Jonson found Shakespeare, now retired at Stratford, at work revising the translation of Isaiah for the Authorized Version of the Bible.

In June 1959 Lewis wrote Eliot, asking him to tell their commission secretary that he had arranged for the committee to meet at Magdalene College that July. He added that he hoped the Eliots would dine with him and his wife, which they did. After Joy's death, Lewis and Eliot continued to keep in touch. A letter from Lewis in 1962 told Eliot not to sympathize too much with his illness because, while it kept him from doing things he wanted to do, it also excused him from doing a good many things he didn't want to do.

In March 1958 the Eliots went to Rome, where he received an honorary degree. Italian students lined the road to the university shouting "*Viva* Eliot!" Eliot told an interviewer that such public acclaim had not meant much to him until he had his wife to share it. That April they went to America where Eliot had the pleasure of introducing Valerie to his family and friends.

Ezra Pound had finally been released from prison and had gone to Italy to live with his daughter. He was beginning to feel he had failed as a poet, so Eliot took pains to keep up their correspondence, reassuring Pound that all modern poets owed him a debt. In the early '60s, Pound's daughter asked the Eliots to come to Italy to celebrate her father's birthday, but Eliot was too ill to travel. He sent instead a congratulatory telegram, in which (as in *The Waste Land*) he again called Pound, in Dante's phrase, *il miglior fabbro*, the greatest poet alive.

Pound in turn suddenly decided that his entire household must reread *After Strange Gods*, and his contribution to the posthumous Tate collection of essays was to call Eliot "the true Dantescan voice" and to urge everyone to READ HIM. As Pound's daughter suggests, their long friendship had involved a great deal of "superficial banter," which led to many stories that do not do justice to the strength of their affection and admiration for each other.

After Eliot's death, when the original manuscript of *The Waste Land* unexpectedly turned up in New York, Valerie Eliot went to Venice to see Pound. He was pleased to meet her and gave her considerable help in deciphering his editorial comments on *The Waste Land* manuscript for the facsimile edition she was editing. Pound commented then that he should not have cut so much of the poem and that Eliot should not have listened to him so much. When a memorial plaque to Eliot was dedicated in the Poets' Corner in Westminster Abbey, the Pounds made the effort to come to London to attend the ceremony and to visit Valerie Eliot.

The Elder Statesman was put on the summer of 1958 in Edinburgh. Although it did well the play did not have a long run in a London theater and it was never taken to New York. Reviewers treated the comedy as a tribute to Eliot's marriage, most of them considering it to be "minor Eliot." Russell Kirk, for example, wrote that few men were given the opportunity to be "surprised by joy" at sixty-eight, and then speculated about whether or not Eliot would have written his major works if he had not endured his unhappy first marriage and its aftermath.

Eliot's seventieth birthday was celebrated at a cast party for the play's opening night in London, as well as with a smaller family party at the

Eliots' apartment the next day. Among the guests was sculptor Jacob Epstein, whom Eliot had gotten to know when Epstein did a bust of Eliot. Eliot told his friends he felt younger at seventy than at sixty and that it was his happiest birthday. In the many interviews brought on by the occasion, Eliot sounded the most relaxed and open he had ever been.

Winter brought on Eliot's breathing problems again. The Eliots went to the West Indies, where they regularly spent part of the winter for the next five years, usually stopping in America to visit family and friends and to make enough appearances to cover their travel expenses.

In October 1959 Eliot returned to Chicago, giving his first poetry reading there to an enormous, appreciative audience at Orchestra Hall. Robert Giroux, who said that Eliot was the easiest author he ever worked with, had commented that he had been startled to realize how nervous Eliot was before a reading, although he always performed well. Giroux had suggested that Eliot should pause between poems because his audience might not know when he had finished one, and this performance showed that Eliot clearly had taken that advice to heart.

The Orchestra Hall reading, preserved on tape by Chicago radio station WFMT, showed Eliot at his most genial, sharing memories and amusement at his own severe young self. He not only reminisced about his American background, but said that if beer had made Milwaukee famous, modern poetry had done the same for Chicago. He paid special tribute to Harriet Monroe who had given him his start and thanked *Poetry* magazine, which was sponsoring his performance.

Eliot commented that a considerable amount of research had gone into the forgotten origins of the name *Prufrock*, but he knew that its yellow fog was St. Louis fog, brought on by burning Illinois's soft coal. After reading the last section of *The Waste Land*, "to relieve the audience's feelings," he read *Ash-Wednesday*. Then, "for shock value," Eliot gleefully followed with "Macavity: The Mystery Cat."

A little later in St. Louis, Eliot read "The Dry Salvages" for the first time beside the Mississippi River. He told his audience that the poem began where he had begun and ended where he and his wife planned to end, in the parish church at East Coker, thus exemplifying both the lines "In my end is my beginning" and "in my beginning is my end."

One of his most famous interviews also took place in 1959. Done at Faber & Faber in London and in New York, it was published in the *Paris*

Review, and later appeared in *Writers at Work* with an introduction by Van Wyck Brooks. It included interviews with others of Eliot's generation like Robert Frost, Marianne Moore, and Ezra Pound. Frost and Eliot had been more adversaries than acquaintances, but Moore and Eliot were old friends. Both were born in St. Louis, went east to college, but met only when they were published poets. Eliot wrote that Moore's poems were part of the small body of durable poetry that had maintained the life of the English language—perhaps the greatest praise he could give anyone.

The interviewer had first talked with Eliot in his small office in Russell Square with its gallery of portraits, ranging from Virginia Woolf to Yeats, Goethe, and Pope Pius XII. There and in New York, Eliot's mood ranged from the wry and ironic to hilarious bursts of booming laughter, making a mockery out of the Eliot caricature as a prim Jeeves, armed with a tightly furled umbrella.

Very much at ease as an elder statesman, Eliot discussed his development as a writer, commenting on what experience and maturity had taught him, but subtly, as he had been doing elsewhere, revising and interpreting his career. Then the interviewer asked if it was true that he now considered that his poetry belonged to the American literary tradition.

In response Eliot agreed that he was sure that his poetry had more in common with his "distinguished contemporaries" in America than anything written in England. Asked if he also thought there was a definite connection with the American past, he explained that his work would not have been the same if he had been born in England, or if he had stayed in the United States. His work was a combination of the two places, but he felt that its emotional springs were American.

As late as 1960 Eliot was still hoping to write another play, but his health, if not his spirit, grew more and more frail. He was at work on a study of poet George Herbert, which he did not manage to complete until early 1962. During the spring of 1961 he gave the address at the University of Leeds called "To Criticize the Critic," in which he rewrote his own critical career.

When he finished the little book on George Herbert, Eliot spent much of his time and energy putting his 1916 Harvard doctoral thesis on F. H. Bradley in shape for publication. As he did so, he told his wife that he no longer understood it. But that was partly the Eliot sense of humor; Bradley's Idealism had greatly influenced his own work. The thesis was published in 1964 with the title *Knowledge and Experience in the Philosophy of F.H. Bradley*.

On the November day in 1963 when American President John F. Kennedy was shot, C. S. Lewis, who was also in very bad health, quietly died, marking the beginning of the end of an era in Christian apologetics. Although Eliot was interested in one "Christendom" and admired Pope John, neither Lewis nor Eliot would have been really at home in the post-Vatican II era symbolized by the Bishop of Woolwich's *Honest to God*, by repetitions of Nietzsche's claim that God is dead, or even by attempts to live Bonhoeffer's "religionless religion."

Careful revisionists with a great regard for the past, Eliot and Lewis would not have cared for proliferating new translations of the Bible or for revisions of *The Book of Common Prayer* that destroyed its public use of "classical" English and "watered down" the faith. Like Chesterton, both of them had helped to preserve classical Christianity in the post-Christian world.

By December 1964 Eliot was very ill, having been in and out of the hospital all fall. He rallied for Christmas, then went into a coma and died on January 4, 1965, just after the Feast of the Circumcision, which he had celebrated in "A Song of Simeon," and just before the Feast of the Epiphany, to which he had given modern currency with "Journey of the Magi." His ashes were taken that spring to St. Michael's in East Coker, where they lie under a memorial tablet that asks the worshiper, "Of your charity, pray for the repose of the soul of T. S. Eliot, poet."

Postscript

To call T. S. Eliot a philosopher poet is a Chestertonian paradox. Its primary purpose is to make readers see the man and his work more clearly, and to make critics open their eyes to see why they may "suspend both belief and disbelief" in Eliot's twentieth-century world view, but must also try to understand it. For in Christian Eliot's own words, from his first essay on Dante, "We are not here studying the philosophy, we *see* it, as part of the ordered world."

Earlier Eliot had expressed the hope that he had "purified the language of the tribe" as well as stated a vision. But because it is often his early, pre-Christian poems that appear in anthologies today, few of his readers come to know Eliot as a Christian believer and social thinker, who was intelligent and imaginative—a true philosopher poet.

To say that a poet's religious commitment is irrelevant to his work, or is only a minor eccentricity, is, in the words of Edmund Fuller, to display an arrogant and "insular complacency." Such an attitude assumes that the world is a place where belief is *impossible*, when believers know that it is a real world where belief is always and forever *difficult*. But Eliot's magnificent showing forth of the dynamics of belief and disbelief, as well as his portrayal of what Nathan Scott has called "civic virtue," have often been dismissed as psychological disturbances. Such a view trivializes his accomplishment. If his work speaks only to his own condition, it has little social relevance or message for the world today.

By refusing to acknowledge or discuss the philosophical and theological presuppositions of Eliot's work, commentators have been able to ignore the public nature of his concerns about society and his continuous posing of philosophical questions: What is Man? What is his duty and his destiny? The fact that Eliot's social and religious thought is more subtle, wise, and humane than the non-Christian world perceives it to be is ignored. The fact that his poetry is a part of "that small body of durable poetry that has maintained the life of the English language" is seen as a contradiction, not an affirmation.

To call Eliot a philosopher poet, however, represents another paradox which might have made him refuse the honor. Unlike the thirteenth century, when Dante could show his readers an ordered vision of their world, Eliot wrote in modern times, when artists had no framework of accepted traditions and beliefs except to create their own. Before and after his conversion to Christianity, Eliot had to keep rebuilding the very tradition he used. The prevailing belief was Conrad Aiken's theme that there is no theme, that there was nothing to hold to in Yeats's "broken center." That difficulty still exists, except that now Eliot himself has become part of the process.

But by using the terms with which he hailed Dante as philosopher poet, Eliot can be shown to belong with Dante. First, Eliot was an attentive student of the art of poetry and a painstaking practitioner of his craft. He was a servant of his language, not its master, who passed on to posterity its own language more refined. Second, Eliot's emotional range in his work expresses everything from depravity's despair to the beatific vision. Finally, in his day Eliot was the most European, the least provincial poet, without ceasing to be local.

Eliot has become a prophet without honor in his own century, a major poet whose preaching is ignored. But seen as a philosopher poet,

Eliot's vision of a Christian life has something to say to our late twentieth-century world. Today theology has become so secular that the intersection of time and the timeless, of the everyday and the mysterious, has lost any sense of the holy. In this age of anxiety, Eliot speaks to that condition. He describes our modern alienation and despair, then offers us the hope of his own "turning."

As a philosopher, concerned with the major issues of civilization—education, community, culture, and tradition—Eliot publicly took positions consistent with his personal piety. He was much criticized for ranking political or social alternatives as good or bad for the community, but the ethical concerns that he raised are still relevant, and undecided, today. Because philosophical questions require redefinition by every generation, we can learn from Eliot's "tentative" solutions. His political views no longer sound quite as reactionary in today's world, where conservatism is again an intelligent option and meritocracy's bureaucrats have run wild. The world is still torn apart by rival ideologies and Christendom is not united, so that Eliot's deep concern about education, its social role, and its cultural transmission, has assumed profound significance for us today.

Eliot described the world we live in. Read within the context of belief, his poetry and his criticism, literary and social, form a unified philosophical outlook that can help us to redeem our time. As a Saul of Tarsus, educated in the academy, who became the Paul who was a citizen of no mean city, Eliot can command our minds and enthrall our hearts, giving us the faith, hope, and charity to "fare forward" as voyagers.

Selected Bibliography

Works of T. S. Eliot
(listed in chronological order)

Prufrock and Other Observations. London 1917.
Poems. London, 1919.
The Sacred Wood. London, 1920.
The Waste Land. New York, 1922.
Poems, 1909-1925. London, 1925.
For Lancelot Andrewes. London, 1928.
Ash-Wednesday. London, 1930.
Selected Essays. London, 1932.
The Use of Poetry and the Use of Criticism. London, 1933.
After Strange Gods. London, 1934.
The Rock. London, 1934.
Murder in the Cathedral. London, 1935.
The Family Reunion. London, 1939.
Old Possum's Book of Practical Cats. London, 1939.
The Idea of a Christian Society. London, 1939.
Four Quartets. London, 1944.
Notes Towards the Definition of Culture. London, 1948.
The Cocktail Party. London, 1950.
The Confidential Clerk. London, 1954.
On Poetry and Poets. London, 1957.
The Elder Statesman. London, 1959.
Knowledge and Experience in the Philosophy of F. H. Bradley. London, 1964.
To Criticize the Critic, and other writings. London, 1965.
Poems Written in Early Youth. London, 1969.

The Complete Poems and Plays of T. S. Eliot. London, 1969.

Selected Prose of T. S. Eliot. New York, 1975.

(For a complete bibliography consult Donald Gallup, *T. S. Eliot: A Bibliography.* London, 1969.)

Selected Secondary Sources

Ackroyd, Peter. *T.S. Eliot: A Life.* New York: Simon and Schuster, 1984.

Booty, John. *Meditating on Four Quartets.* Cambridge: Cowley Publications, 1983.

____. *Three Anglican Divines on Prayer, Jewel, Hooker, and Andrewes.* Cambridge: Cowley Publications, 1978.

Browne, E. Martin. *The Making of T.S. Eliot's Plays.* London: Cambridge University Press, 1969.

Bush, Ronald. *T.S. Eliot: A Study in Character and Style.* New York: Oxford University Press, 1984.

Carpenter, Humphrey. *The Inklings.* London: George Allen & Unwin, 1978.

____. *W.H. Auden: A Biography.* London: George Allen & Unwin, 1981.

Cavaliero, Glen. *Charles Williams: Poet of Theology.* Grand Rapids, MI: Wm. B. Eerdmans Publishing Company, 1978.

Dale, Alzina Stone. *Maker and Craftsman: The Story of Dorothy L. Sayers.* Grand Rapids, MI: Wm. B. Eerdmans Publishing Company, 1978.

____. *The Outline of Sanity: A Life of G.K. Chesterton.* Wheaton, IL: Harold Shaw Publishers, 1982.

Davies, Horton. *Worship and Theology in England: The Ecumenical Century, 1900-1965.* Princeton, NJ: Princeton University Press, 1965.

Davies, Walford (tape). *Imagination and Belief in the Poetry of T.S. Eliot.* Wheaton College: Writing and Literature Conference, 1980.

Edel, Leon. *Bloomsbury, A House of Lions.* New York: Avon, 1979.

Ellmann, Richard. *Eminent Domain.* London: Oxford University Press, 1967.

____. *Goldon Codgers, Biographical Speculations.* London: Oxford University Press, 1973.

Frye, Northrop. *T.S. Eliot: An Introduction.* Chicago: The University of Chicago Press, 1963.

Fuller, Edmund. *Man in Modern Fiction.* New York: Random House, 1958.

Gardiner, Helen. *The Art of T.S. Eliot.* London: Faber & Faber, 1949.

Gordon, Lyndall. *Eliot's Early Years.* Oxford: Oxford University Press, 1977.

Griffin, William. *Clive Staples Lewis, A Dramatic Life.* San Francisco: Harper & Row, 1986.

Hadfield, Alice Mary. *Charles Williams.* New York: OxfordUniversity Press, 1983.

Hastings, Michael. *Tom and Viv.* New York: Penguin Books, 1984.

Highet, Gilbert. *People, Places, and Books.* New York: Oxford University Press, 1953.

Howard, Thomas. *The Achievement of C.S. Lewis.* Wheaton, IL: Harold Shaw Publishers, 1980.

Howarth, Howard. *Notes on Some Figures Behind T.S. Eliot.* Boston: Houghton Mifflin, 1964.

Jones, David E. *The Plays of T.S. Eliot.* London: Routledge & Kegan Paul, 1960.

Kenner, Hugh. *The Invisible Poet.* London: Metheun & Company, Ltd., 1965.

Kojecky, Roger. *T.S. Eliot's Social Criticism.* New York: Farrar, Straus & Giroux, 1971.

Kirk, Russell. *Eliot and His Age.* New York: Random House, 1971.

Levy, William Turner and Victor Scherle. *Affectionately, T.S. Eliot, 1947-1965.* Philadelphia: J.B. Lippincott, 1968.

Lewis, C. S. *The Abolition of Man.* New York: Macmillan, 1947.

_____. *The Pilgrim's Regress*. London: Geoffrey Bles, Ltd., 1933.

_____. *A Preface to Paradise Lost*. London: Oxford University Press, 1942.

_____. *Reflections on the Psalms*. New York: Harcourt, Brace & Company, 1958.

Linton, Calvin (tape). *Diligence Observed in Eliot's Cocktail Party*. Wheaton, IL: Writing and Literature Conference, 1985.

Malvern, 1941: The Life of the Church and the Order of Society. London: Longmans, Green & Company, 1941.

March, Richard and Tambimuttu, editors. *T.S. Eliot: A Symposium*. Chicago: Henry Regnery Company, 1949.

Matthews, T. S. *Great Tom: Notes Toward the Definition of T.S. Eliot*. New York: Harper & Row, 1973.

Matthiessen, F.O. *The Achievement of T.S. Eliot*. New York: Oxford University Press, 1959.

Meyers, Jeffrey, editor. *The Craft of Literary Biography*. New York: Macmillan Company, 1985.

Moorman, Charles. *The Precincts of Felicity*. Gainesville, FL: University of Florida Press, 1966.

Muggeridge, Malcolm. *The End of Christendom*. Grand Rapids, MI: Wm. B. Eerdmans Publishing Company, 1980.

Nott, Kathleen. *The Emperor's Clothes*. Bloomington, IN: Indiana University Press, 1958.

Patrick, James. *The Magdalen Metaphysicals*. Mercer, GA: Mercer University Press, 1985.

Pickering, Kenneth. *Drama in the Cathedral: The Canterbury Festival Plays, 1928-1948*. Worthing, West Sussex: Churchman Publishing Ltd., 1985.

Pike, James. *Modern Canterbury Pilgrims*. New York: Morehouse-Gorham Company, 1956.

de Rachewiltz, Mary. *Discretions*. Boston: Little, Brown and Company, 1971.

Sayers, Dorothy L. *Begin Here*. New York: Harcourt, Brace & Company, 1941.

_____. *The Mind of the Maker*. New York: Harcourt, Brace & Company, 1941.

Schwartz, Sanford. *The Matrix of Modernism: Pound, Eliot, and Early Twentieth-Century Thought*. Princeton, NJ: Princeton University Press, 1985.

Scott, Nathan A., Jr., editor. *Man in the Modern Theatre*. Richmond, VA: John Knox Press, 1965.

_____. *The Broken Center: Studies in the Theological Horizon of Modern Literature*. New Haven, CT: Yale University Press, 1966.

_____. *The Poetry of Civic Virtue: Eliot, Malraux, Auden*. Philadelphia: Fortress Press, 1973.

Sencourt, Robert (pseud). *T.S. Eliot: A Memoir*, edited by Donald Adamson. New York: Dodd, Mead, 1971.

Simpson, Alan. *Puritanism in Old and New England*. Chicago: University of Chicago Press, 1955.

Spender, Stephen. *T.S. Eliot*. New York: Penguin Books, 1975.

Tate, Allen, editor. *T.S. Eliot: The Man and His Work*. New York: Delacorte Press, 1966.

Walsh, Chad. *The Literary Legacy of C.S. Lewis*. New York: Harcourt, Brace, Jovanovich, 1979.

Williams, Charles. *The Descent of the Dove*. London: Faber & Faber, 1939.

Writers at Work: The Paris Review Interviews. New York: The Viking Press, 1961.

(For a thorough discussion and listing of critical works about Eliot, see Canary, Robert H. *T.S. Eliot: The Poet and His Critics*. Chicago: American Library Association, 1982.)

Index